There's no question that fear is the greatest obstacle for millions of people, and it's holding them back from discovering their ultimate purpose in life. That's why Jackelyn Viera Iloff's new book, *What If You Could? Find Faith in the Face of Fear*, is so timely and important. I've known Jackelyn for decades, and she's one of the boldest people I know. Her confidence is remarkable, and it has opened amazing doors in her life. So if you're hesitant to seize the moment, fearful of the future, or simply nervous about your next step—this book is for you. You'll never look at your future the same way again.

—PHIL COOKE, PhD, filmmaker, media consultant,
and author of *One Big Thing: Discovering
What You Were Born to Do*

Fear strangles our lives, and we're often caught in its web without even realizing it. That's why Jackelyn Viera Iloff's new book, *What If You Could? Finding Faith in the Face of Fear*, challenges our thinking about what's holding us back and shows us a powerful escape route. What are you waiting for? Read it today! You'll never be the same again.

—KATHLEEN COOKE, cofounder of Cooke Pictures
and The Influence Lab; author of *Hope 4 Today:
Connecting with God in a Distracted World*

What If You Could? breaks down what it means to live in faith with unwavering clarity. As I read it, I experienced inexplicable tears, followed by gales of laughter and joy. I faced past sorrows, I welcomed forgiveness into my heart, I let go of

crippling doubts, and I looked my "fears" straight in the eye. I felt grace, love, and connection—all more strongly and deeply. This book is an unfettered account of all that God needs us to understand about faith. The question "What is faith, and how do I live it?" is more meaningful than "What is the purpose of my life?" As when we understand and embrace faith, the purpose of our life is illuminated. *What If You Could?* is one of the most practical and spiritually empowering books of the last decade.

—GABRIELLE ALLEN, film and television producer, director, marketing and media strategist, entrepreneur, speaker, and philanthropist

Jackelyn Viera Iloff's book, *What If You Could? Find Faith in the Face of Fear*, is sure to be an encouragement to those seeking a real faith that can overcome real fear. Jackelyn shares unique insight that is sure to reach those seeking a faith-filled life. This book is a must-read.

—JAY SEKULOW, chief counsel, American Center for Law & Justice

Jackelyn has written a timely book for such a day as this. There is so much news and information around to create fear, but we find her sharing about finding faith in the face of fear. The stories she tells revolve around confronting fears but not on your own. Jackelyn has seen that when God calls us to do something, we need to trust Him because He has the best in mind for us. Be inspired and encouraged to see God take the "impossible" and turn it into the "I'm possible" by immersing yourself in this book and in the thirty-day faith-building verses.

—Peter Irvine, PhD, author, speaker,
and cofounder of Gloria Jean's Coffees Australia

What If You Could? is a tremendous help in reminding us that God is there to help us in all that we undertake to do. Fear stands in the way, but faith in God causes us to excel and have peace. I salute you, Jackelyn, for a job well done!

—Dodie Osteen, cofounder of
Lakewood Church, Houston, Texas

Jackelyn Viera Iloff has given us a blueprint, a personal manifesto that is so needed for those of us who have at one time or another been hamstrung by fear. I encourage you to not just read this great book, but sit with it, internalize it, and then apply its lessons to achieve the dreams God has in His heart for you.

—Reverend John Gray, associate pastor,
Lakewood Church, Houston, Texas

I love the title of this book, *What If You Could?* It communicates so eloquently how a faith-centric life can withstand the onslaught of the fear that permeates our personal and national narratives—a fear that has become the grid through which many people interpret how they live their lives. With keen biblical insights and personal stories, my friend, Jackelyn, helps illumine how a practical faith, centered on God's Word and obedience, is the antidote to this obsession. Read this book! And release fear's grip on your life!

—JOE BATTAGLIA, president of Renaissance Communications and author of *The Politically Incorrect Jesus*

Jackelyn Iloff's book, *What If You Could?*, presents an understanding of faith in a simple, straightforward expression that will bring you to the core understanding of faith and how to appropriate it. I was struck at how many times I read something I already "knew," but it resonated in such a way that it refreshed my spirit and comforted my soul. As you read this book, it's important to understand this is not a theoretical effort. I've known Jaceklyn for many years—this is how she lives her life.

—JERALD BROUSSARD, managing director, Growth Advisors International, LLC

I believe this book will inspire you to turn away from fear-based thinking to live a life full of joy. Jackelyn brings God's words to life through her stories and insights.

—ROMA DOWNEY, actor, producer, and president of LightWorkers Media

I know *What If You Could?* will be an encouragement and free many people to succeed in life.

— REVEREND CATHY DUPLANTIS, editor-in-chief of *Voice of the Covenant* magazine, television co-host, and senior pastor of Covenant Church, greater New Orleans

WHAT IF YOU COULD?

Find Faith in the Face of Fear

Jackelyn Viera Iloff

BroadStreet
PUBLISHING

BroadStreet Publishing Group, LLC

Racine, Wisconsin, USA

BroadStreetPublishing.com

WHAT IF YOU COULD? *Find Faith in the Face of Fear*

Copyright © 2018 Jackelyn Viera Iloff

ISBN-13: 978-1-4245-5560-4 (softcover)

ISBN-13: 978-1-4245-5561-1 (e-book)

Stock or custom editions of BroadStreet Publishing titles may be purchased in bulk for educational, business, ministry, fundraising, or sales promotional use. For information, please email info@broadstreetpublishing.com.

Cover design by Chris Garborg at garborgdesign.com

Typesetting by Katherine Lloyd at theDESKonline.com

Front cover author photo by Eric Forsythe at forsythefotography.com

Printed in the United States of America

18 19 20 21 22 5 4 3 2 1

Contents

Foreword

By Joel Osteen

Without a doubt, fear is one of the most common yet destructive emotions we face. It is the enemy of our faith, oftentimes showing up when we face unpredictable situations like severe health issues, overwhelming financial difficulties, or failing relationships. If we are not mindful, fear can rush in and engulf us at a time when we need our faith the most. It is also the enemy of our destiny, paralyzing us and keeping us from reaching our dreams.

One time, a young lady approached me in great emotional distress asking for prayer. She had just been accepted to an Ivy League school, and she expressed to me her fear that if she enrolled in the school, she would be unable to compete with the smarter students. I knew the young lady's family and was well aware of her academic achievements and extensive community service. She was a perfect candidate, yet she was filled with so much fear and doubt that she was seriously considering not taking advantage of the greatest opportunity of her young life. I prayed with her and then told her, "Both God and the school know your achievements and both of them think you're smart enough." She replaced her fear with faith and not only attended the school but graduated with honors.

Faith and fear have something in common: they both ask us to believe in a future that we cannot see. One asks that you believe that only bad things lie ahead, while the other asks you to believe that God holds you in the palm of his hand. One asks you to believe that nothing good comes from your present situation; the other asks you to trust in a God who promises you hope and a future. Clearly, these two futures cannot exist together; therefore, we must choose the one that will live in our spirit.

This is what David did when he said, "I sought the Lord, and He heard me, and delivered me from all my fears" (Psalm 34:4 KJV). When he spoke these words, David was being hunted by King Saul whose army was intent on killing him. Did he fear? Yes. But, he chose to replace that fear with faith and believe that God had a great plan for him. Notice that David does not say God delivered him from Saul, but that God delivered him from all of his fears. This was the important first step in allowing God to bring about David's destiny. Ultimately, as we all know, David prevailed in his struggles and became the greatest king ever to rule over Israel.

The Bible says that God did not give us a spirit of fear but of power and love. This is an important Scripture for each of us to get down in our spirit, and it is a centerpiece of this book. In the twenty-five years that I have known Jackelyn Iloff, I cannot remember ever seeing her act out of fear. Yet, throughout her book, she speaks honestly about the many times she was forced to confront her fears, find her place with God, and allow Him to bring peace to her spirit. Her struggles, while private and hidden from view, were intense and real. Jackelyn is living proof that if you reach out to God in your time of worry, He will replace that spirit of fear with one of power and love and bring you to the destiny that He has planned for your life.

1

THE POWER
OF FAITH

But without faith it is impossible to please Him,
for he who comes to God must believe that He is,
and that He is a rewarder of those who diligently seek Him.

HEBREWS 11:6 NKJV

When I was a young woman, I had an opportunity to move from California to Washington, DC, to work on a presidential re-election campaign. I was thrilled at the idea of crossing the country and setting out on my life's adventure as an adult. My future seemed bright.

From the time I was a little girl, God had given me an interest in politics. I used to sit with my dad and his friends while they debated the political issues of the day. I even piped in from time to time with my own opinion, and Dad and his friends smiled and said I was destined to be a lawyer some-day. That was their way of saying I was precocious.

However, when the time came and a real offer was in front of me, I felt torn. I had never been away from my family. Three generations of strong women raised me. My great-grand-mother, a wise, loving, patient woman who loved children and teaching, taught me at an early age the love of cook-ing. She helped me learn to read and write in two languages before I entered first grade. My grandmother was a modern role model, a smart and driven woman, a single mom, and the breadwinner for her family during a time when women were only seen as homemakers. My mom is and has always been someone I could count on as a steady influence in my life, a person who relies on her faith for everything.

But I am more like my dad in so many ways. We shared a love of politics, history, science, and good food. He taught me to stand up for myself and to be a responsible person. He convinced me I was capable of achieving anything I set my mind to do. And he showed me what it means to have a heart for those who are less fortunate.

The thought of leaving my family to set out on my own was exciting—but I was stuck as I pondered what might lie ahead. I didn't want to leave my younger sister and brother either. I liked being their big sister and being available for them. I loved all my family. How could I leave them behind?

And yet I had been given the opportunity of a lifetime—to work in a political campaign and subsequently in the administration.

But what if I failed? How could I hold my head up if I came back with my tail between my legs? What if I was supposed to stay in California? What if I was getting in over my head? After all, I was going to a place where everyone had multiple degrees and was extremely well connected. I had none of that. My thoughts and fears were defeating me.

I had never shied away from making decisions. I'd had no trouble deciding where I would go to college, who I should date, which sorority to join, what classes to take, or for which jobs to apply. But this decision to leave California, which I thought had everything I could ever want, was a very big leap.

I prayed for an answer, but I wasn't allowing myself to hear it in faith. I was stuck in the fear of, "What if I couldn't?"

So I went to my parents' house and sat on the bed with my mom. "What should I do?" I asked. She replied, "Go. If you don't like it, you can always come back. But you'll never know what God has for you if you don't try."

That was exactly what I needed to hear. I packed up two suitcases with as much as they would hold, and on January first, I landed at Dulles International Airport in Washington, DC, ready to start my new adventure.

I never looked back.

That moment totally changed the path I was on. It led me to a huge change in my life and, as result, also affected other people's lives.

I was asked to serve in the re-election campaign of one of the most admired and faith-filled presidents of our lifetime. I went on to serve in President Ronald Reagan's administration at the US Department of Transportation and was part of the public affairs team that established the widespread use of the three-point seat belt and third-brake-light safety initiatives.

I have had many God-led opportunities to meet and work with highly regarded national leaders throughout my career. However, the best thing that happened to me while living in DC was that I met my husband and had my first child. And all of it happened because I stepped out in faith.

God has taken me places most people only dream of going, simply because I said, "Yes, Lord." All the things I've accomplished happened because I took that first step even though I was anxious and fearful.

The more I relied on my faith, the more I succeeded. I have learned over my life that God is always faithful to His Word. Once I stepped out in faith, He was not going to leave me unarmed for battle. There were battles along the way, but in this fallen world we will always encounter battles.

He led me to two mighty men of God, Christian teachers John Osteen and Kenneth Copeland, and others who taught me how to stand on the Word of God and believe for what it said about me. I learned what it means to believe for what I pray. God has all the answers. He knows the end from the beginning, and He wants us to commune with Him so we can have all the promises that are in the Bible for us. Faith IS everything!

Faith is the key to accessing all that God has for us in His kingdom. Jesus said in Mark 9:23, "If you can believe, all things are possible" (NKJV).

Notice He says, "If you *can* believe." Not if you *will* believe, or if you *want* to believe. He says, "If you are able to believe … really believe." So if we don't believe, if we operate in fear instead of faith, we cancel the possibilities. Faith is the opposite of fear.

Hebrews 11:6 says that without faith, it is impossible to please God. Without faith you can't operate in His authority. We were created in the image of God. Until Adam and Eve walked away from God, we had power and authority from God. Through Jesus Christ we can reclaim that authority, but only through faith.

Can you even begin to imagine what God is sharing with us? Over and over He tells us how to live in victory while we live in this fallen world. And yet His words just wash over most of us, having no real impact because we haven't studied His Word.

What if you really understood all that faith requires of you and all that faith delivers to you? All that faith is in you.

God is all-powerful and He is working on your behalf. He is fighting off powers and principalities that would hinder you. He is protecting you from evil. When you stand in faith, you can stand boldly and ask for whatever you need, knowing that He will fulfill those needs because you are His child. It means that He will dwell inside you if you allow Him.

First Chronicles 29:11 says, "Yours, O LORD, is the greatness and the power and the glory and the victory and the majesty, for all that is in the heavens and in the earth is yours.

Yours is the kingdom, O Lord, and you are exalted as head above all." And if He lives in you, through faith, you can accomplish mighty works.

Having access to faith means you don't have to believe the lies of the enemy or live bound by your inability to answer God's calling. Your faith will allow you to do all that God has called you to do. You can use all the gifts He has given you and be victorious.

If you knew how powerful faith is, you would never allow fear or doubt to control you.

When God created the world, He spoke it into being. He created humans as spirit beings of light, to live in relationship with Him forever. When you walk in fear and turn away from God, you walk in darkness. When you accept the power of God's faith in you, you no longer live in darkness.

The Bible tells us in 1 John 5:4 that we have the victory because of our faith. God is telling us that your faith is the victory! God's plan has always been to grant you all authority and power. He made us in His image so that we could reign on this earth and do what He can do.

What if you could learn to use your faith to face your fear, to cast out doubt and unbelief, to break through to success and peace, and to do all that you are called to do in this life? Well, if you can believe all that God has told us about faith, then I believe you can live a successful life. With faith, you as a child of God are "thoroughly equipped for every good work" (2 Timothy 3:17 NKJV).

What Are You Afraid Of?

How often have you heard yourself say some of these things?

- I'm afraid I can't do that.
- I'm not smart enough.
- I'll never lose that extra weight.
- I am terrified of flying.
- I'm scared of heights.
- I don't believe I will have enough money this month to pay the bills.
- My health isn't what it used to be.
- My blood pressure is going to be the death of me.
- I am scared to go out on my own.
- I am frantic over my child's problems.
- I am so mad at myself for not getting that promotion.
- I will never be good enough.
- I can't do it. I just can't.

God's Word says we should "fear not." Yet fear, anxiety, and unbelief are part of our everyday lives.

Deuteronomy 31:6 says, "Be strong and of good courage, do not fear nor be afraid of them; for the LORD your God, He is the One who goes with you. He will not leave you nor forsake you" (NKJV). And yet we sit in the darkness, contemplating ruin, afraid to step out of the boat, paralyzed by the thought of failing.

If you knew how
powerful faith is,
you would never
allow fear
or doubt
to control you!

Failure is not the end; it's just a stepping stone to success. But you must believe that you will succeed and achieve your goals. It's only through faith and a strong relationship with God that we can accomplish all that we are called to do.

If it is impossible to please God without faith, then without faith, you cannot operate in his authority. You were created in the image of God, and until Adam and Eve walked away from Him, we operated with authority given to us by God. You and I can reclaim that power, but only through faith in Jesus Christ—100 percent, sold-out, "I can move mountains" kind of faith.

When you speak fear instead of faith, you create an environment where your unbelief rules your life. Instead of getting into God's Word to displace the anxiety you feel, you might go see a scary movie, sit down with a pint of ice cream, go to the bar to have a drink, step outside to have a smoke, or whatever it may be that soothes you. But feeding yourself fear and defeat is never going to enable you to succeed.

In the first book of the Bible, Genesis, God asked the human beings He created, "Why are you hiding?" They answered, "Because we were afraid." Because of their disobedience, they feared God. If they had remained faithful, they would have lived a blessed, success-filled eternal life. Jesus Christ had to come to earth and die for this sin so that we could be restored to living out our eternal lives in faithful relationship with God.

If you believe what God has promised, and you believe His Word, why do you walk in fear? In Genesis 15:1, God says to Abraham, "Fear not … I am your shield; your reward shall be very great."

Do you view the Bible as a historical narrative, a nice story, or a handbook? Many people can quote the Bible chapter and verse, but haven't a clue what God is saying to them about the power and authority they have when they walk in faith.

As you practice speaking in faith over your life, you allow God to use you, to bless you, and to make you a blessing to others. Every word that comes out of your mouth holds the power of life or death. What are your words calling forth in your life, and in the lives of your children, your spouse, your neighbors, and your local, state, and national leaders?

Don't Put Your Faith in Fear

Are you putting all your eggs in one basket—a basket of fear? What are you feeding on every day? What is it that you're putting into your mind, your spirit, and your soul? Are you asking God to help you with your life every day? Or are you limiting Him to Sunday mornings and the dire calamities that come along in life?

I know a woman who claims to be a God-fearing, church-going person. But when I ask her, "How are things going with you?" she tells me all the things that aren't going right and how she needs prayer to get out of the latest mess in her life. When I ask her what she's believing God will do, she tells me, "I just pray for God to have mercy on me and hope He finds me worthy."

Clearly, she is not fully aware of the kind of relationship God wants to have with her. If she were, she would know He has a better opinion of her than she has of herself.

She obviously doesn't understand the lack of power in that kind of "faith." She believes in God the way children believe in Santa Claus or the Tooth Fairy. Just make a wish, say a prayer, and keep hoping in vain it will come true.

Folks like that believe that, "If I just hold on, God will save me from this hell that is my life." But God can't do what you won't allow Him to do. If you put up a wall, don't be surprised when nothing gets through.

When Adam and Eve ate of the tree of knowledge, they essentially told God, "We can figure out this life without you." They realized, too late, that they couldn't. We have a tendency to do the same thing. We plead with God to save us when all we have to do is give ourselves back into God's hands and let Him work good in our lives.

If you put your faith in a fear-based relationship with God, you have turned away from all that He has made you to do. You have turned off the personal communication He wants to have with you, and you have cast yourself adrift in a very scary storm.

In Luke 8:25, after Jesus calmed a storm the disciples feared would drown them, He asked the men, "Where is your faith?" They marveled, saying to one another, "Who then is this, that he commands even winds and water, and they obey him?"

Is your faith adrift in a storm, and you have no idea how to get out of it? Instead of continuing to fear the circumstances, get into relationship with God. Seek His best for the situation. Ask Him to stop the storm. Then you have to do your part to fix the problem. Call it dead or resolved, fixed or mended, and stand on that as fact. Pray for God to bring about peace and understanding, to get things back on track.

You may be required to put in some hard work, or you might see a supernatural turnaround. It may require a miracle from heaven, but God will answer you, and He will work everything out for your good.

Talk About Your Faith

Now that you can see how important it is to walk in faith, stop talking about fear and start talking about accomplishments and possibilities, and believe in the mission God has set on your heart. Get into the Word, read the Bible, and listen to messages that affirm how to use your faith.

Proverbs 3:5–6 says, "Trust in the LORD with all your heart and lean not on your own understanding; in all your ways submit to him, and he will make your paths straight" (NIV). Practice affirming what you believe about God and what He has for you.

Stand on these promises from Scripture:

- "I can do all things through Him who strengthens me" (Philippians 4:13 NASB).
- "God gave us a spirit not of fear but of power and love and self-control" (2 Timothy 1:7).

- "'I know the plans I have for you, declares the LORD, plans for welfare and not for evil, to give you a future and a hope. Then you will call upon me and come and pray to me, and I will hear you'" (Jeremiah 29:11–12).

When you hold close the promises of God and do not waver in unbelief, you will grow stronger in faith, give glory to God, and be "fully assured that what God has promised, He was able also to perform" (Romans 4:21 NASB). You will become more faith filled and less fearful.

In Luke 12:32, Jesus tells us, "'Fear not, little flock, for it is your Father's good pleasure to give you the kingdom.'" You can count on God's promises.

Good Things Can Happen

When you listen to God and pray faithfully, you get into a habit of talking to Him all day long. I pray often, and I taught my daughters to pray from a very young age.

When my girls were little, I stayed home with them. I enjoyed dressing them up like angels and princesses; making up stories for them; singing songs little kids sing; creating fun themed birthday parties; taking them to the zoo, the children's museum, and the beach; and teaching them new things. Life was good.

One September morning when my daughters were both less than five years old, our country came under attack, and then the Gulf War began in Iraq. The daily news was filled with stories of battles and devastation.

News correspondents reported on shortages that hospitals were experiencing because of so many injuries. They focused on a little girl about five or six. In the States, her injuries would not have been life-threatening. But because of the lack of basic supplies like sterile bandages and antibiotics, she was in danger of losing her life.

My girls were healthy and happy and safe. I could only imagine the injured girl's parents helplessly standing by, not able to do anything to take care of their daughter. Something inside me cried out to God, *Please, Lord, don't let that child die.* And as I was walking away from the television, I heard Him say, "So what are you going to do?"

Lord, what can I do? I have no way to help that child.

"Yes, you do. I have given you all you need to help the people in Iraq."

When I thought about it, I realized He was right. I knew lots of people. So I called my doctor friends, who gave me the names of medical supply charities. I called political leaders I knew and government agencies I had worked with while in DC, and that got me to the next step of gathering medical supplies—medicine, bandages, syringes, wheelchairs, crutches, and even X-ray machines. I found donors to pay for the shipping costs, and we found the right hands in Iraq to accept the shipments.

If you have ever dealt with government red tape, international shipments, and trying to reach the proper person in some faraway bureaucracy to get something done, you know this could have been a complicated and daunting task that took months or got stopped by lack of proper documents. But I believed that God had called me to the task.

Every time I called an office or tried to reach a key contact, the right person answered. There was never any red tape. Even when I had to reach overseas contacts in different time zones, I connected with people who assured me that the medical supplies would reach those who needed them. I witnessed a miracle straight from God.

I will never know whose lives were saved because of those supplies reaching the war-torn country of Iraq, but God does. And He gave me one of the greatest gifts of my life by using me to save the lives of people I will never meet in a country I may never visit.

This experience changed how I saw myself in God's eyes!

I have never been more clear that God was doing a new thing in me. I matured in my faith because I was open to Him asking me to use the gifts and talents He had given me to do His will.

As you can see, He is no respecter of persons. He used me to help someone in a far-off country. You too can be used by God, if you stop talking about what you can't do and believe that *you* can do all things through Christ who strengthens *you* (Philippians 4:13). Let God bring about good things in and through you!

2

FAITH LIKE A MUSTARD SEED

---○---

Then the disciples came to Jesus in private and asked,
"Why couldn't we drive it out?" He replied, "Because you
have so little faith. Truly I tell you, if you have faith
as small as a mustard seed, you can say to this mountain,
'Move from here to there,' and it will move.
Nothing will be impossible for you."

MATTHEW 17:19–21 NIV

What does it mean to have faith like a mustard seed? Are you supposed to believe that you can do all things if you believe with just a little bit of faith? Or does it mean that like a mustard seed, you have all you need inside you to grow your faith into a mighty tree that bears fruit, and that your faith is powerful?

I think you know the answer. You are powerfully and fully equipped with His Holy Spirit, and you have the ability to bring forth your hopes and dreams by calling on His holy Word, if you live according to His will.

I had two grandfathers I didn't know well. One passed away before I was born, and the other passed away when I was in high school, but he lived far away and I only saw him two or three times in my life. However, both of these enigmatic forefathers passed onto me a wonderful gift: the love of words and stories. You see, they were both journalists.

My paternal grandfather started one of the first luxury automobile magazines of his day in the 1920s. He was the publisher and editor, along with being an entrepreneur and politician. My maternal grandfather was a sports writer, political pundit, and author of several books. So with that legacy, it was natural for me to become a communications major in college and have a career in which writing has played an important role. I have written articles, speeches, reports, short stories, and ministry lessons ... but never a book (until now), even though I always had the desire to write one.

God gave me a dream, but life events kept taking priority. I had a lot on my plate. But that desire kept raising its head, especially when my girls were young. When they had friends or cousins come over and I wanted to keep them entertained or get them to bed, I made up stories about clouds, teddy bears, princesses, or whatever they named. I even wrote a sonnet about King David for them. It was so much fun!

Once my kids were grown, I had a bit more time on my

hands. So I began preparing lessons to teach in our church's women's ministry. One of the lessons was on how to face fears, and that really sparked something inside me. So I sat down with some friends who had written books and started asking questions. Then I tried to formulate a book outline. I asked every author I knew how they had gotten published. But I kept feeling like I was trying to look over a fence and I wasn't tall enough to get a good view.

Knowing I have a faithful God, and having faith that He will do what He called me to do, I kept trying to move forward. I researched and wrote a more extensive outline for the book. But nothing was happening in my quest for a publisher. Finally, I just put the manuscript away and trusted that God would show me when His timing was right.

At the beginning of the new year, I went to a conference I attend almost every year. It's a good way for me to stay in touch with friends and colleagues in media ministries. The conference had an exhibit hall filled with vendors, including publishers and book sellers, so I went looking for more information, figuring maybe I had been doing this wrong. I walked around the hall, talking and learning, but felt like I was going in circles. So I went back to my room and had a conversation with God. "Lord, please show me what to do. If you want me to write this book and get it published, it has to be done by you. Thank you, Lord, for taking care of this."

I left my room, and as soon as I walked off the elevator, I saw a friend I hadn't seen in a while. As we caught up on each other's lives, she told me she had left her previous job and had just started working with a publisher who was seeking new writers. Before I could think, I blurted out, "I'm writing a book." The next thing I knew, I was talking to the publisher and they said they wanted to publish my book. God is faithful, amen!

As this wonderful dream unfolded in front of me, I realized that I had been the stumbling block. I thought I had to do it under my own steam when really I just had to get out of the way. God already knew what the book would say and when it would be printed and sold. He knows who is meant to read it and how it will bless them. It doesn't get any better than that!

Faith is everything. And having a relationship with our Lord is what leads us to victory.

When we seek the Lord and understand His divine law, we will understand how faith works. The Bible tells us to ask and it shall be given, knock and it will be answered, seek and it will be revealed. In other words, we are to pursue God and look to Him for everything.

If you truly understood all that faith allows you to do, according to your faith you would be able to affirm the presence and power of God until the very substance of His Spirit would appear right in front of you. Hebrews 4:12 asserts, "The word of God is living and powerful, and sharper than a two-edged sword, piercing even to the division of soul and spirit, and of joints and marrow, and is a discerner of the thoughts and intents of the heart" (NKJV).

First Corinthians 4:20 tells us that the kingdom of God does not consist of words only; it has the power of life and death. And the power of faith in cooperation with God allows us to bring forth the substance of things hoped for, of things not seen. It can move mountains. It can change the course of your life.

God brought forth my dream because I sought Him and believed He would resolve any stumbling blocks in the way. He is faithful to His Word and to His creation, which is you and me! We also have to be faithful in order to reap His benefits.

King David's Faith

God can overcome the smallest and greatest challenges in your life. He does that through your heart and through your God-given abilities.

In 1 Samuel 16:7, the Lord spoke to Samuel about David when he was still a shepherd, saying, "'Do not consider his appearance or his height. ... The LORD does not look at the things people look at. People look at the outward appearance, but the LORD looks at the heart" (NIV). He was saying that He knows what is inside a person and how to use that for His glory.

God knew who David was, who he would become, and how he would serve the Lord. He used those things to make a shepherd a great man of God. First Samuel 16:18 says David was "a son of Jesse of Bethlehem who knows how to play the lyre. He is a brave man and a warrior. He speaks well and is a fine-looking man. And the LORD is with him" (NIV).

David fought lions and bears before he faced his battle with Goliath. He fought them and developed his faith in God. As a young man, he came to understand that even when people fail, God does not fail. God remained the same every time David called upon Him.

King David's faith was built on knowing that he could always call on God and that God would answer. He constantly and consistently asked God for His will, especially when it came to significant political or military matters. Many people know of David's slingshot and the one-on-one encounter with the Philistine giant Goliath. But he dealt with other battles of the mind and body as well. If you read 1 and 2 Samuel and Psalms, you will see the trials and tribulations that this man of God faced during his lifetime.

David's faith allowed him to believe God's promises and that God would determine the method and the timing to fulfill them. If you trust God and allow Him to do things His way, you can be certain that His way will fulfill His promises.

God's Faith Defined

By now you might be asking, *What is faith?* The Bible contains a clear definition in Hebrews 11:1: "Now faith is the assurance of things hoped for, the conviction of things not seen" (NRSV). Simply put, the biblical definition of faith is trusting in something you cannot explicitly prove.

So how much faith do we need? God does not require much of you—just that you believe in Him completely. Believe that you are His and that you are better with Him than apart from Him.

Romans 10:17 says, "Faith comes from hearing [what is told], and what is heard comes by the [preaching of the] message concerning Christ" (AMP). If you're not studying the Word of God and hearing about His promises, you won't know what your rights are as His creation. So how can you pray in faith? How can you know His will for your life? How can you birth what you cannot conceive?

If God is concerned with the lives of sparrows and the lilies of the field, why wouldn't he be even more concerned about you and me?

He's got me right where He wants me to be. He has me in places where I can be His light to the world. Where does God want you to be? Have you sought out His will for you?

Hebrews 11:1 says, "Now faith is the assurance of things hoped for, the conviction of things not seen." In other words, the fundamental fact of existence is this trust in God, this faith, the firm foundation under everything that makes life worth living. It's our assurance of what we can't see in the natural world.

God sees you as a beautiful creation, completely fulfilled in everything He could possibly package in you. If faith as small as a mustard seed can move mountains, it's not because faith is a small thing but because it's complete in its power. As a believer, you should have abundant faith! You should know how to use your faith. You should be able to affect many things in this world.

If you could do anything, what would you do? If you woke up tomorrow and truly believed that God was going to bring your heart's desire to you, what would you do?

Are You Afraid of Change?

Most people like to have a routine. It makes them feel safe. Doing the same thing, when it's successful, assures you that you have the right formula. But if that formula is not working, is not in line with God's will, or is no longer under the anointing, then believing in that formula is a false hope.

Some people are afraid of any kind of change—even having something different to eat for lunch or moving the furniture around or changing their hairstyle. The fear of change causes you to get stuck. But change is inevitable. Things will change, so why not make it so it goes in your favor?

Changing things requires faith that the new circumstances will bring good or better results than before. Here is where good decision making and using wisdom are essential.

What if you got a promotion, and you changed the way things were being done in a way that benefitted the people who worked at your organization or the people who bought goods or services from your company?

What if you invented the next great app? A mom recently created an app called Baby Tracker that enables mothers to chronicle everything about their babies, from feedings to diaper changes to growth milestones to medical appointments. A woman had the idea and then had the faith to act on what

The purpose of
affirming your faith
with positive words
is to train your mind
to think differently
and to speak with
power and purpose
about what you
believe God will
provide for you and
through you.

she thought she could do, and now people are benefiting from that great idea.

What if you stopped eating junk food and started eating healthy foods and creating tasty, nutritious meals for yourself and your family because you had the faith that God would help you lose weight? What if you started a blog and shared your ideas with other healthy-minded people? You could perhaps save lives in ways you may never know.

Think about what you are called to do, what your faith will allow you to step out and change. Think about how using your faith to overcome fears of failure could create a new path for your life.

Many of our presidents were successful farmers, lawyers, generals, teachers, or scholars. One was an architect and inventor, another a film star, and some were wealthy entrepreneurs. If you have read about their lives, you can see they all felt a compelling calling. They wanted to change the way things were done.

So against all odds, conventional thinking, and the naysayers, they set out to win the highest office in the nation. And they did! Why? Because they believed in their gifts and in their dreams. They never thought about how to lose.

Like He did in David, God saw in these men the heart of a lion and said, "Okay, you have my anointing as long as you do this for my people." And it's not like everyone got behind them 100 percent when they made the decision to run for office. I'm sure there were people along the way who said, "Do you really think you want to run for president? Do you know what you're getting yourself into? What if you don't win?"

But they didn't think that way. They didn't listen to negative voices of unbelief. They believed they could do it, and each one set about doing what he knew to do, having faith in the outcome and in his convictions. Many of the presidents and candidates I have known or have studied have had great faith and not many moments of self-doubt.

We are all capable of greatness and of doing extraordinary things. Though not everyone will be famous or celebrated, every human being has the promise to become an instrument of God. Don't live your life in quiet desperation, forgetting you are an anointed child of God. Don't let your light be obscured because you're hiding it under a basket. Have faith in your outcome.

The Enemy Wants You Stressed Out

Why do you not believe that you can do all things through Christ who strengthens you? The enemy wants to deceive you so you fall short of your potential. Ever since the garden of Eden, Satan has been deceiving us. You have to guard your mind and your heart against fear, doubt, and unbelief, because it's a wedge to separate you from Christ.

In Matthew 8, we read that Jesus got into a boat and his disciples followed him: "And behold, there arose a great storm on the sea, so that the boat was being swamped by the waves; but he was asleep. And they went and woke him, saying, 'Save us, Lord; we are perishing.' And he said to them, 'Why are you afraid, O you of little faith?' Then he rose and rebuked the winds and the sea, and there was a great calm. And the men marveled, saying, 'What sort of man is this, that even winds and sea obey him?'" (verses 23–27).

Another time, in John 6:16–21, the disciples found themselves on the sea and a storm rose up. This time Jesus was not in the boat with them. But as the disciples were filled with fear, Jesus came to them, this time walking on the water. He asked Peter to step out of the boat. Peter trusted Jesus and stepped out on the water—until he realized what was happening, and at that moment he took his eyes off Jesus. And he began to sink.

If you want God to do something supernatural for you, you have to take that step of faith. You hold the key to your success. God offers you His hand to accomplish it, but you can't take your eyes off Him.

Your faith has to be independent of any circumstances or conditions. Keep your focus on God's will. Trust in your relationship with Jesus Christ. As soon as you take your eyes off Him and look at your circumstances, you will sink.

In the late 1990s, my husband and I moved into our first house. It had three trees in the front yard— beautiful, tall, old oaks that had grown there since the 1950s when the house was built. In Houston, we have a lot of windy thunderstorms, and my daughters' bedrooms were toward the front of the house. Something in my spirit concerned me about those trees, so I prayed, *Please, Lord, take care of my children whenever they sleep in their rooms, and keep those trees away from the house when it storms. Let no branches come down on the house. If the trees are to fall, let them fall away from the house.*

During a five-year period, several bad storms came through, including a tropical storm and a hurricane. Each of the trees had its own problems, and one by one they fell as their roots got waterlogged and the winds came against them. The last one came down right across the front yard in slow motion. But none of them fell on or near the house. I kept my eyes on Him. God was faithful, and the trees did what God commanded. I believed that when the storms came, God would answer my prayers and protect my home and my family. I had faith in His promises.

Never do I want to have God say to me, "O, you of little faith." I want him to say, "Well done, good and faithful servant!" God's promises have always given me strength.

When I was a little girl, whenever storms came, my family would tell me it was God moving the furniture in heaven, so I never feared storms. As I grew older and began to realize the power of my faith, I often asked God to take care of the weather, and He has been faithful on so many occasions. As I matured, I would call out to the thunder and lightning to be still, fully believing that it would calm down and go around me.

He staved off bad weather for my September wedding in the Caribbean (during hurricane season) and gave me a picture-perfect day. He held off the rain at a small outdoor concert I had planned in Detroit as part of my church's community outreach. The rain clouds just swerved around us like we were in a bubble. One night, a storm caused thunder and lighting to crack right over my house, with one clap so loud it rattled the windows and woke me up. I said peace to the storm, and it instantly quieted down and moved on.

Not every time do storms cease or move on with little effect. When we had a Category 4 hurricane go through Houston, I prayed, along with lots of Houstonians, that the storm would not hit with full force, that it would spare our house and neighborhoods from serious damage. Still, there were tragic losses as a result of the hurricane's force. But we also experienced the kindness of others, the love of our neighbors and friends, and even the care perfect strangers showed to each other. God's love in us helps to bind our wounds and reaffirms our faith in each other! So even though the events were monumentally devastating to millions of people, God brought forth healing in us and through us because of our love and compassion. His love in us binds our wounds and heals our spirit.

You see, it's not that storms won't come; it's that storms won't break you if carry His Holy Spirit in you!

Don't Believe the Enemy

Don't let the enemy tell you it's okay to speak words of unbelief. You may not think your words mean anything. But if you keep repeating and believing in the same negative words over and over, those negative things will surely come to pass.

Sometimes your spoken words are the opposite of your dreams and desires. They can even be in conflict with your prayers. Your prayers have no power because your words of unbelief reveal your lack of faith. When you speak with purpose, you are giving instructions to spiritual forces to bring about things here on earth.

The purpose of your affirmations is not to "blab it and grab it." Wishing won't make something appear, won't make you lucky, and won't magically bring about what you need. Expecting prosperity to just drop out of the sky or appear on a winning lotto ticket is not how you will truly prosper or succeed.

The purpose of affirming your faith with positive words is to train your mind to think differently and to speak with power and purpose about what you believe God will provide for you and through you.

Second Corinthians 10:4–5 says, "The weapons of our warfare are not carnal but mighty in God for pulling down strongholds" (NKJV). You have the power to destroy arguments and every lofty opinion raised against the authority and knowledge of God and to take every thought captive to obey Christ. If you are in a relationship of faith with God, you have the power to destroy strongholds!

Change Your Thinking

The more you depend on circumstances or conditions, however favorable the situation may be, the less you are trusting in God's promise of "believe that you receive" (Mark 11:24 NKJV).

Now it's easy to believe when life is good. But when circumstances get off on the wrong track, doubts can creep in and faith can be hard to maintain. But doubt isn't going to get you into the king's palace, or to the Fortune 500 boardroom. And it sure won't allow you to be the best parent to your kids, or a caring child to your parents, or even bring about a complete healing.

We need to believe God's Word and see the outcome we believe He has for us from the beginning, never wavering from that confidence that it will happen as the Lord has determined it should be—for our good.

Esther had faith that took her from being an orphan, with no prospects for a worthwhile future, to living in the palace and becoming an instrument of God's will for His people. Because of her devotion and willingness to listen to His guidance, she became queen, and through her, God saved the Jewish people in Persia from devastation and destruction.

Faith played several roles in the story of Esther:

- Mordecai, Esther's uncle, knew that God wanted to save the Jewish people from death through him and his adopted daughter Esther. So when an opportunity arose, he acted without hesitation.
- In the middle of trying to decide what she could do to help her people, Esther didn't allow fear to paralyze her. Instead, she fasted and prayed and

believed that God would deliver her to the right place at the right time. Ultimately, it became clear she had only one choice: to approach the king. She knew she had been chosen "for such a time as this" (Esther 4:14) and that God would find someone else if she declined. So she took a leap of faith, leaving the outcome with God.

- The king believed and trusted his queen. He had complete faith in Esther, based on his love for her. He trusted her to make decisions that would be in his best interest and for the well-being of his subjects.

In dealing with the turmoil of the situation, Esther realized she couldn't allow fear to paralyze her. Instead, she left the outcome with God. She prayed and fasted, seeking His will. It was clear she had only one real choice, and that was to face the king and take whatever came. Esther's faith, Mordecai's belief, and the king's willingness to trust his queen saved the Jews because they each had the courage to act according to God's will. This is a great example of how we should trust God too.

3

FAITH
ISN'T FAIRY DUST

---○---

God is able to make all grace abound to you,
so that having all sufficiency in all things at all times,
you may abound in every good work.

2 CORINTHIANS 9:8

aith connects you with God, but faith does not magically give you whatever you want. You can't just wish on a star or a birthday candle and expect all your troubles to disappear. If you are begging and pleading with God to just wave His hand and do something to change your circumstances, you will never get the answer you need, want, or deserve.

Your relationship with God is not based on fairy tales or superstitions but on fact and reality. Faith is based on the trust you have in Him, the confidence that He is the everlasting I AM.

The Bible tells us that faith is the true manifestation of our relationship with our Creator. It is not simply believing the stories about Him, because "even the demons believe" (James 2:19 NIV).

Faith is trusting what you cannot see and believing that God is working with you to bring it about for your good. Faith provides the substance and essence of a relationship with God. Your power and authority is grounded in your faith. Every day in every way, you need to make the decision to believe Him.

You also have to be obedient to His calling and His warnings. Isaiah 30:21 says, "Your ears shall hear a word behind you, saying, 'This is the way, walk in it,' when you turn to the right or when you turn to the left."

One day a friend of mine, a woman who prays daily and believes God has His hand on her, was leaving her son's school and was headed to the office where she worked. She drove a big seven-seater SUV that held all her kids, their friends, and their gear. But that morning she was alone in the car. As she was about to turn right toward the freeway, she heard God say, "Don't get on the freeway." It was such a strong impression that she obeyed without question and turned left instead.

Just then, her husband called and asked if she would grab something he had left at the house. Since she was still nearby, she did as he requested. After stopping at the house, she headed back toward work. Out of habit, she took her usual route to work, forgetting that God had told her not to get on the freeway.

Not one minute past the freeway entrance, a car slowed down abruptly to change lanes. The car behind it slammed on his brakes. My friend put on her brakes too, but the heavy SUV could not stop before it hit the car in front of her, which struck the first vehicle. Fortunately, traffic had been heavy and they were only moving along at about forty miles per hour, so no one was hurt. There was just a lot of bent metal.

My friend spent the next few days dealing with police reports, insurance claims, and repair shops. And chastising herself for forgetting God's warning not to take the freeway. The results could have been worse, but God's angels were watching over her and kept her and everyone else from being badly hurt. But she regretted allowing herself to get so distracted that she failed to remember what God told her.

Even a small disobedience can affect your life. But don't turn away from God just because He didn't spare you from the consequences of your own bad decision. Instead, press into God even more. Ask for forgiveness, seek His mercy, and stand on His promises. Then listen and obey, and always act on His advice.

Decisions, Decisions

Every decision you make can create problems or successes. Most times the consequences don't amount to much. You wore a red hat instead of a blue one, and the red one made you look bold and sassy—good outcome. You used half-and-half in your latte instead of cream, which made the coffee taste just as good with fewer calories—good outcome.

Sometimes your decisions can lead to wonderful things happening in your life. You went out on a crazy date set up by your best friend and met "the one" you ended up marrying—happy ending. You saved up for a new car, then waited for the year-end sales, and the expensive showroom model you'd been admiring, even though it was way over your budget, becomes available as a pre-owned vehicle for an amount within your budget—an answer to prayer.

But some decisions lead to bad outcomes.

You put off changing the tires on your car (even though the tread was worn), you drove down the highway anyway, and the tire shredded and came off the rim. You lost control of the car and ran off the road. Or maybe you got accepted at two different colleges, but the one you chose didn't lead you to the life you envisioned. You began to drink occasionally, but then you ran into a bad patch and it became a bad habit. Now it is making you sick and you need radical intervention in order to survive. These are examples of wrong decisions that brought about undesired results, but God did not send them down as punishment. They are the result of bad decisions.

God gave us a free will to make our own choices. But those choices have consequences. If you seek God diligently and strive to make the right decisions with Him, you will have good outcomes. If you make bad decisions (such as eating unhealthy foods, doing drugs, abusing alcohol, incurring crushing financial debt, or getting into the wrong relationships), the results will catch up with you. Even though God didn't send those things to you, you can trust God to help you and ultimately have a better outcome.

Luke 6:43–45 says, "No good tree bears bad fruit, nor again does a bad tree bear good fruit, for each tree is known by its own fruit. For figs are not gathered from thornbushes, nor are grapes picked from a bramble bush. The good person out of the good treasure of his heart produces good, and the evil person out of his evil treasure produces evil, for out of the abundance of the heart his mouth speaks."

Sometimes we can't see what might have happened if we had made a different decision, but we know the choice was pivotal for our lives. Robert Frost's poem "The Road Not Taken" illustrates that concept. In this beautiful poem, Frost looks down two paths in the woods, a crossroads if you will. One path is well worn and the other seems less traveled. He knows that as soon as he chooses one over the other, he will not likely pass that way again. Ultimately, he chooses the road less traveled. And looking back from some future point, he acknowledges that it made a tremendous difference in his life.

You also have choices, and when you choose faith over fear, anxiety, or stress, you can count on God's Word and truth to manifest in you.

Everyday and in every way you need to make the decision to believe Him!

Ruth's Decision

In the book of Ruth, Orpah kissed her mother-in-law good-bye, but Ruth clung to her. "And [Naomi] said, 'See, your sister-in-law has gone back to her people and to her gods; return after your sister-in-law.' But Ruth replied, 'Do not urge me to leave you or to return from following you. For where you go I will go, and where you lodge I will lodge. Your people shall be my people, and your God my God. Where you die I will die, and there will I be buried. May the LORD do so to me and more also if anything but death parts me from you'" (Ruth 1:15–17). When Naomi realized that Ruth was determined to accompany her, she stopped trying to change her mind.

That was a pivotal moment for both women. Ruth's decision to go to Bethlehem with Naomi set in motion actions that were fulfilled in generations to come. Ruth became King David's great-grandmother and ultimately an ancestor of Jesus Christ Himself.

What role will your faith have in your life and the lives of future generations?

When you decide to stand on faith, fear may still raise its ugly head. Even Jesus, who had perfect faith, fell to His knees in the garden of Gethsemane and asked God for help because He feared what was ahead. God sent an angel to give Jesus strength. God loves you too, and He will give you strength to move forward.

If you're not seeking God and relying on Him, fear will

become a stronghold in your life. Don't just say you believe. Trust with all your might that God will be the resolution to all your problems.

Are you believing for God's best or what you think is best for you? They're not always the same thing. But through prayer, fasting, journaling, or whatever other means you choose to use to find the will of God for your situation, the Holy Spirit will lead you to the right choice.

To Move or Not

Several years after I moved to DC, God asked me to trust Him again for the next chapter in my life. I was in the perfect place in my career: Mid-Atlantic Public Relations Director for a major accounting firm. I'd just had my first child, my husband and I had a bid on a brand new, two-story, three-bedroom townhouse, and life was looking good.

Then one day my husband told me, "I've been offered a job back home in Houston and I want to take it." I was dumbfounded. How could he ask me to leave my friends, colleagues, and a good-paying job I loved in the most powerful city in the world and go to a city where I knew no one, with no assurance of a job and no immediate prospects of a home?

I told him I would pray about it. I didn't want to go, but I wanted to be obedient to God's direction. After much prayer, I told my husband, "I will agree on one condition. If my company has my same position open in their southwest regional office, I will know this move is from God."

As it turned out, they did. I interviewed, and the company agreed to transfer me.

But the first two years were rough. My husband and I and our two-year-old child were living in a one-bedroom apartment. Then, shortly after moving to Houston, the firm I worked for changed their headquarters to Dallas, and since we didn't want to make another move, I lost my position with the firm.

I didn't realize then where God's path would lead me. So I prayed and sought Him more than I ever had. And even though His ways were ultimately more than sufficient, it was a season of faith building faith like I had never known.

Faith pleases God, and He is a rewarder of those who seek Him. Throughout that time in my life, I kept believing that His path for me was where I would flourish. Eventually, we bought a nice house and had another child. During this season, I experienced some of the best moments in my life and some of the most challenging ones. I focused on being a good mother for my sweet girls, and I really enjoyed being with them as they grew up. It was a treasured time in my life.

But I missed working and the rewards of seeing projects through to a successful conclusion. In Washington, DC, I had been involved in high-level decision making, and my husband and I frequently went to corporate and political events. I was on the board of several organizations, and we had lots of social activities on the weekends. It was fun and very exciting.

Now, living in Houston, I felt isolated. Sunday was the only time we had the opportunity to socialize with family and a few close friends. I wasn't part of any organizations outside the grade school my girls attended. But in that season of reflection, because of my relationship with God, my faith got me through and I grew stronger.

I dove into my new role as full-time mother. I hosted overnight pajama parties and became homeroom mom and soccer coach. I learned to cook healthy gourmet meals, did some gardening, and read all that I could about faith and prayers. I filled up on the Word of God. With my family I attended church services on Wednesday night, Sunday morning, and Sunday night. God was raising me up.

That season was like watering a seed that had broken ground but had not yet fully bloomed. But God knew where I was going, and I knew He was going to help me get there the best way possible.

As I met new friends in Houston and joined organizations, I started to make an impact again. When the girls grew older and needed me to hover less, I started doing public relations consulting. God brought back to me the things I had set aside. He restored and revived long-lost friendships and associations I had cherished in Washington and California. Not a thing I went through was wasted. Everything was brought full circle.

When you allow God to be first in your life, "all things work together for good" (Romans 8:28).

4

FEAR ATTRACTS WHAT YOU FEAR

---○---

The thing that I fear comes upon me,
and what I dread befalls me. I am not at ease,
nor am I quiet; I have no rest, but trouble comes.

JOB 3:25–26

Have you ever noticed that when you focus on something you're afraid might happen, it often does? You say to yourself, *Whatever you do, don't spill that water on the antique table,* and inevitably you're going to spill it. That's the "law of dread": the thing you fear will happen because your whole being is focused on it.

Job lived for years in fear and dread of bad things happening. He was so sure his children were doing something evil, he offered up sacrifices to stave off the bad things he just knew were going to occur (Job 1:5). He was consumed with fear that his children were going to curse God and he would lose everything as a result. Job's fear became a magnet that attracted the very thing he feared most. God did not lift his hedge of protection; Job's fear did.

If you stand on faith and have confidence in God's Word, you'll attract what God has for you. Romans 10:10 says, "With the heart man believeth unto righteousness; and with the mouth confession is made unto salvation" (KJV). Just as heart-belief and mouth-confession of God's Word brings about the blessings of salvation, having fear in your heart and speaking it out loud brings destruction. You have to guard your thoughts or your mouth will ruin your blessings.

Fear Pollutes Your Thinking

Fear cripples your faith and stifles God's ability to work in your life. When you rely on your own devices to determine what's good for you, the enemy will come in with his agenda to destroy you. The choice is not between good and evil, because no true Christ-follower would intentionally choose evil. The choice is between faith in God's plans or the fear-based plans you try to implement yourself, which are really plans you allow the enemy to bring about in your life.

The more you hold on to your fear, the more you'll gain what you don't want. It becomes a habit—a bad habit that perpetuates the problems. But when you act on God-filled faith, your outcomes gain in strength. One good decision leads to the next, and success manifests according to God's will.

Any time you are fearful, call on your faith to rise up within yourself. As Proverbs 3:5–6 says, "Trust in the LORD with all your heart and do not lean on your own understanding. In all your ways acknowledge Him, and He will make your paths straight" (NASB).

Fear Is Not from God

Isaiah 55:8–9 says, "My thoughts are not your thoughts, neither are your ways my ways, declares the LORD. For as the heavens are higher than the earth, so are my ways higher than your ways and my thoughts than your thoughts."

Fear is not a godly characteristic. In fact, 2 Timothy 1:7 says, "God has not given us a spirit of fear and timidity, but of power, love, and self-discipline" (NLT). Fear and timidity come from another source, and it should not be acknowledged, agreed with, or given any power.

Fear drains your faith. When the Israelites had the option of going into the promised land, they heard that giants occupied the land, and because of their fear said they would not go on, and then judgment came. God called them an evil generation because of their fear and disobedience (Dueteronomy 1:28–35).

When was the last time you allowed fear to hold you back, to make you timid, or to steal your confidence? Luke 16:10 says, "'Whoever can be trusted with very little can also be trusted with much'" (NIV). Show God that you trust Him every day, that you know who you are in Him, that you will walk with Him in confidence, and that you know you can do all things with His strength.

You have authority. Not using that authority doesn't do you any good. Embrace it! You don't have to live saddled with fear, anxiety, and anger. You can live victoriously.

Where the Battle Begins: Fear vs. Faith

Child development research tells us that humans are born with two innate fears: the fear of falling and the fear of loud noises. These fears are necessary for protection and survival. All other fears are learned from the environment we live in and the circumstances or situations we experience.[1]

So if you are living in fear, it's a cage of your own making, created by your inability or unwillingness to live in faith. The more you do something, the more it becomes a habit. Living in fear is a bad habit. And because bad habits usually provide some type of "benefit" in your brain chemistry, it's difficult to eliminate them. But you can override any habit by replacing it with a new one.

According to Sydney-based science journalist Signe Dean, researchers from the University College London in 2001 examined the new habits of ninety-six people over the space of twelve weeks and found that the average time it takes for a new habit to stick is 66 days, although individual times varied from 18 to 254 days. "The take-away message here is that if you want to develop a new behavior, it will take at least two months, and you shouldn't despair if three weeks doesn't do the trick—for most people that's simply not enough. Stick with it for longer, and you'll end up with a habit you can keep without thinking."[2]

Psychologist Timothy Pychyl, PhD, says, "Breaking a habit really means establishing a new habit." He recommends estimating a minimum of six months, "and that's only if you're committed to the change and you are conscientious in your practice of a strategy for change."[3] Neuroscientist Elliot Berkman states, "It's much easier to start doing something new than to stop doing something habitual without a replacement behaviour. ... People who want to kick their habit for reasons that are aligned with their personal values will change their behavior faster than people who are doing it for external reasons such as pressure from others."[4]

To take authority over your thoughts and habits, write down the Scriptures that empower you and give you solid ground to stand on. Then speak them in faith. Proverbs 18:21 says, "Death and life are in the power of the tongue, and those who love it will eat its fruit" (NASB).

I used to tell my girls, when they were acting out, to use their words to tell me what they needed. God wants you to use your words to defeat fear and walk in faith. That is why we need to watch our words as well as our thoughts. In Mark 11:20–24, Jesus tells us that our words have the power to cast mountains into the sea and wither fig trees. James 3:5 tells us, "The tongue is a small member, yet it boasts of great things."

All we really
need to do is turn
toward God and
rely on his love,
because perfect
love casts out
all fear.

To illustrate the power of words, try this experiment. Take three small plants, give them all exactly the same soil, light, and water. Use sweet words to encourage one to grow, yell discouraging words at the other one, and treat the third one like you would any ordinary plant. After a week or two, you should see a marked difference in the plants. The third plant will be growing normally. The one you encouraged to grow will be taller and more robust. The other one will be smaller and less vigorous.

If a plant reacts to your words and the emotions behind them, imagine what impact your words have on your own spirit. When you dwell on fear, you limit your growth.

Turn your circumstances over to God and submit yourself to His perfect will. Then you can overcome fear, anxiety, and self-defeating thoughts. And you can change your circumstances with the power of faith.

Psalm 56:3 says, "When I am afraid, I put my trust in you." Keep that verse in front of you always. Don't be fear filled. Be faith filled. You really are as wonderful and powerful as God made you.

Breaking Faith

There are two principles that undergird faith: belief and forgiveness. If you can't or won't believe and forgive, your ability to act in faith's power and authority will be stifled.

Unbelief

If you want to live a success-filled life, unbelief is the number-one stumbling block you'll have to eradicate. Even

Jesus had to deal with the unbelief of others. According to Matthew 13:58, unbelief stops the power of faith cold.

In Mark 9:22–29, Jesus spoke to a man with a child who was deaf and had seizures. The man said to Jesus, "'If you can do anything, have compassion on us and help us.' And Jesus said to him, 'If you can'! All things are possible for one who believes.'" He was telling them their own faith could drive out the demons if they had only believed. Then, "Immediately the father of the child cried out and said, 'I believe; help my unbelief!' And when Jesus saw that a crowd came running together, he rebuked the unclean spirit, saying to it, 'You mute and deaf spirit, I command you, come out of him and never enter him again.'"

Jesus knew where His authority was and how to use it effectively. He helped the people believe by showing them that with faith they could achieve their desires. When the boy's father yelled out, "I believe," he was saying to Jesus, "I put my son in your hands."

The story continues, "And after crying out and convulsing him terribly, it came out, and the boy was like a corpse, so that most of them said, 'He is dead.' But Jesus took him by the hand and lifted him up, and he arose. And when he had entered the house, his disciples asked him privately, 'Why could we not cast it out?' And he said to them, 'This kind cannot be driven out by anything but prayer'" (which according to *Strong's Concordance* is translated to mean "intercession").

In other words, they didn't have the faith to stand in for the child and ask on his behalf. They needed to get right with their faith before they could cast out the demons. They had to get *face-to-faith* with God. They had to understand their faith in God's authority.

Jesus was teaching His followers that the components of prayers spoken in faith are power-filled. Speak it, ask God to be in the midst of it, and give praise and thanks to Him that you will receive it.

Even though the apostles had been watching Jesus and believed in Him, they had no idea what to do. It was as if they had been watching him use an iPhone, but when He handed it to them, they couldn't figure out how to turn it on.

Clearly, Jesus did not think the apostles were ready to pray with the understanding and authority of God. Their lack of understanding the power of their faith made their directives to the demons impotent. They had not filled up sufficiently with God's power and authority to be able to stand against the enemy.

Unforgiveness

God will not tolerate unforgiveness or hard-heartedness. He forgives us over and over, no matter how many times we ask, because He loves us. But if we can't forgive others, we cannot command His power and authority.

Jesus explained this through the parable of the unforgiving servant:

> Peter came up and said to him, "Lord, how often will my brother sin against me, and I forgive him?

As many as seven times?" Jesus said to him, "I do not say to you seven times, but seventy-seven times. Therefore the kingdom of heaven may be compared to a king who wished to settle accounts with his servants. When he began to settle, one was brought to him who owed him ten thousand talents. And since he could not pay, his master ordered him to be sold, with his wife and children and all that he had, and payment to be made. So the servant fell on his knees, imploring him, 'Have patience with me, and I will pay you everything.' And out of pity for him, the master of that servant released him and forgave him the debt. But when that same servant went out, he found one of his fellow servants who owed him a hundred denarii, and seizing him, he began to choke him, saying, 'Pay what you owe.' So his fellow servant fell down and pleaded with him, 'Have patience with me, and I will pay you.' He refused and went and put him in prison until he should pay the debt. When his fellow servants saw what had taken place, they were greatly distressed, and they went and reported to their master all that had taken place. Then his master summoned him and said to him, 'You wicked servant! I forgave you all that debt because you pleaded with me. And should not you have had mercy on your fellow servant, as I had mercy on you?' And in anger his master delivered him to the jailers, until he should pay all his debt. So also my heavenly Father will do to every one of you, if you do not forgive your brother from your heart." (Matthew 18:21–35)

God wants us to operate as He does, and if we can't forgive, we are not acting in love toward others. Unforgiveness will pollute your heart, your words, and your spirit so you can do no mighty works.

Getting past deep hurts is difficult. On your own and without the power of the Holy Spirit, you may not be able to forgive the horrible things that were done to you. But when you seek God, He will give you grace and fortify you. Let Him bring down those strongholds.

In John 20:22–23, Jesus breathed on the disciples and said, "'Receive the Holy Spirit. If you forgive the sins of any, they are forgiven them; if you withhold forgiveness from any, it is withheld.'" In Matthew 6:12, Jesus taught them to pray to the Father, "'Forgive us our sins, as we have forgiven those who sin against us'" (NLT). Lack of forgiveness is a big stumbling block to receiving God's power.

According to the Oxford online dictionary, *forgive* means "to stop feeling angry or resentful toward (someone) for an offense, flaw, or mistake."[5] The Bible teaches that unselfish love is the basis for true forgiveness, since love "does not take into account a wrong suffered" (1 Corinthians 13:5 NASB).

How to Forgive

By forgiving someone, you are not condoning the wrong or acting as if it never happened. Forgiveness does not require you to overlook cruelty. It just requires you to let it go so you will not be poisoned by it. The Bible advises us in Psalm 37:8 to "let go of anger, and leave rage behind" (GW).

Forgiving others is key to receiving God's forgiveness for our own sins (see Matthew 6:14–15). Matthew 10:8 says, "Give as freely as you have received!" (NLT). Proverbs 4:23 tells us, "Keep your heart with all vigilance, for from it flow the springs of life."

The Bible advises us in Psalm 37:8 to let go of anger and abandon rage. Unforgiveness is self-consuming, filling us with darkness. Forgiveness detoxes the mind and spirit. Give yourself permission to not be consumed by the pain. Trust that God will bring the person who hurt you to justice (see Hebrews 10:30–31). When you forgive others, and even yourself, you cancel the hold that unforgiveness has over your mind and your heart.

Ephesians 4:30–32 states, "Do not grieve the Holy Spirit of God, by whom you were sealed for the day of redemption. Let all bitterness and wrath and anger and clamor and slander be put away from you, along with all malice. Be kind to one another, tenderhearted, forgiving one another, as God in Christ forgave you."

5

FEAR DEFEATS YOU BEFORE YOU BEGIN

---○---

*"We have this treasure in jars of clay, to show
that the surpassing power belongs to God and not to us.
We are afflicted in every way, but not crushed; perplexed,
but not driven to despair; persecuted, but not forsaken;
struck down, but not destroyed."*

2 CORINTHIANS 4:7–9

Fear can defeat you before you begin, and it can discourage you from acting in a positive way. It brings despair and defeat. When you are afraid and don't want to appear weak, you may mask your fear with anger. However, if we learn from our failures, we can use our successes to defeat fear.

Fear Is the Opposite of Faith

Fear turns your victory into defeat. It poisons your mind so that you can't have conversations with God. You just sit and whine to God, "How can this terrible thing be happening? Why won't you fix it?"

The enemy keeps whispering in your ear, "You are a loser. What did you expect? You will never amount to anything. God doesn't care about you. You don't deserve his blessings. Who do you think you are? You are bad to the bone. You are not worthy." These lies are meant to turn you away from God, defeat you, and destroy you. Don't listen to them.

Fear paralyzes you. Just like the huddled apostles in the boat not believing in the miracle that just occurred in front of their eyes, you too can have such weak faith that it can't stand the blows of unbelief. If you want to stand strong in your faith, you need to reinforce it daily to strengthen your spirit.

"Not you. You can't do that. Nobody's ever done that with your kind of background. No one is going to take you seriously. What do you know? How can you think like that? You don't have that kind of money. You didn't even finish school." Do these messages sound familiar? These are the tapes that play in your head—or worse, the things well-meaning family and friends say to try to bring you "back down to earth" because they're afraid you will waste your time or money pursuing foolish dreams. They feel like they should warn you. But really they are just speaking unbelief.

Don't listen to the naysayers! Instead, listen to 1 Corinthians 2:5 and rest not "in the wisdom of men but in the power of God."

While growing up, everyone dreams of being successful—as a dancer, writer, teacher, lawyer, engineer, chef, elected official, doctor, entrepreneur, mother, father, or whatever. As adults we want to have a nice home, drive a new car, enjoy good health, take care of our families, be recognized for our achievements, serve others, and live long enough to see our children's children.

But if you allow yourself to become vulnerable to the voices of fear, you will be paralyzed. Fear stops the process of achieving and defeats you before you even have a chance to fail. Don't listen to the voices that say you can't. Because what if you could?

Even in failure you can learn from what happened and become successful. According to inventor Thomas A. Edison, "Many of life's failures are people who did not realize how close they were to success when they gave up."[6] Their faith ran out just at the point they needed it most.

I recently watched a TED Talk on education and innovation. It featured a thirteen-year-old boy who had been contemplating what to do for a science project. After buying a new TV, his family threw away the Styrofoam packaging, which is not easily recycled. So he and his friends set about trying to find a way to efficiently recycle it. Since Styrofoam is carbon based, they figured they might be able to return it to a biodegradable state. They performed several experiments that didn't work out. At one point, while trying to get the fire hot enough to burn down the Styrofoam, they accidentally set Dad's barbecue grill on fire.

Just as they were about to give up, they found a way to reduce the plastic to carbon, which can be used in water filtration systems. They ended up solving two environmental issues and winning the science competition.[7]

That teenager and his partners could have given up after the first try. Or the tenth. But their faith in themselves and their ideas took them through from beginning to end. That kind of never-give-up faith, coupled with God's power, can change the world.

When you believe with all your heart and soul that God is a rewarder of those who seek Him, your power-filled faith can accomplish what you want. If you allow fear to fuel your thoughts, and turn away from God and His best for your life, then your faith is dead and can't accomplish anything.

How can you develop a living faith that conquers your fears? Romans 10:17 says, "Faith comes by hearing, and hearing by the word of God" (NKJV). Hearing and reading God's Word are the most important things you can do to develop a strong faith. God wants you to know Him and completely rely on His direction for your life. Through the everyday practice of hearing, reading, and meditating on Scripture, we develop a strong, confident faith that stamps down worry and fear.

Second Corinthians 3:16–17 says, "When one turns to the Lord, the veil is taken away. Now the Lord is the Spirit, and where the Spirit of the Lord is, there is liberty" (NKJV). Spending time in prayer and quiet worship creates a relationship with God that will see you through even the most difficult paths. When we turn away from Him, we sin, which is being out of the will of God, out of His plan. Fear keeps us focused on fear, not faith.

At different times throughout your day, affirm your faith in God. Your thoughts and prayers will bring forth the blessings He has for you! Second Corinthians 4:13 says, "Since we have the same spirit of faith according to what is written, 'I believed, and therefore I spoke,' we also believe, and therefore speak" (NKJV).

Dwell in the Holy Spirit

When Jesus left this earth, he sent us a Helper, the Holy Spirit. I constantly call on the Holy Spirit for discernment. When I have asked Him to speak through me in important meetings, I have been astounded at what came out of my mouth.

John 14:26 says, "The Helper, the Holy Spirit, whom the Father will send in My name, He will teach you all things, and bring to your remembrance all things I have said to you" (NKJV). Romans 15:13 says, "May the God of hope fill you with all joy and peace in believing, that by the power of the Holy Spirit you may abound in hope."

First Corinthians 6:19 says, "Do you not know that your body is a temple of the Holy Spirit within you, whom you have from God? You are not your own." Second Timothy 1:14 says, "By the Holy Spirit who dwells within us, guard the good deposit entrusted to you."

Each of us has a unique calling. Some are called to be presidents, some to lead organizations, some to preach, some to be caregivers of children or elderly parents, and still others are called to touch the lives of the poor and sick. No matter your calling, if you focus on faith and not fear, God will work through you to reach the world.

My friend Paul is a gifted surgeon who had a thriving medical practice in Little Rock, Arkansas. Though originally from Houston, he had lived in Arkansas for twenty-five years. Paul liked his life in Little Rock. He enjoyed the quietness of the countryside and the small-town feel of his community. He was the head of surgery and had terrific partners. His patients loved and depended on him. He was very involved with his local church and led a vibrant Bible study home group. He and his wife and five children lived in a magnificent antebellum home on several acres in an affluent part of town.

Though outwardly he looked and acted like he was on top of the world, a small voice inside started nagging at him. He felt no peace in what he was doing, but he didn't know where God was leading him. For months he prayed and sought God, but there was no answer to the persistent feeling that there was something else he should be doing.

His father, who led a large church in Texas, passed away from chronic renal failure, leaving the church and his family in a quandary as to what would happen to his ministry. Paul came home for the funeral. As he was driving back home to Arkansas, Paul heard God say, "Give up your practice, move to Houston, and help your family."

Don't listen to
the voices that
say you can't,
because what if
you could?

Now Paul grew up in a faith-filled, loving home, and he had spent his life in obedience to God. But he liked things well ordered and planned. Was God really asking him to leave all that he knew, everything he had achieved, with no planning or preparation? And what was he supposed to help with? It made no sense to his head. But it spoke to his heart.

When he told his wife that he felt like God wanted them to move to Houston, that sparked some discussion. Finally, Jennifer replied, "If that is what God is asking us to do, then we should obey."

So that's what they did. For a while Paul helped wherever he could. But he wasn't practicing medicine, something he had studied and trained for, and had been doing successfully for years. In this season, God was doing a work in Paul, preparing him for what was to come.

Just when Paul thought he would never practice medicine again, he got a call from a doctor he knew in Africa who needed a break. The doctor asked if Paul would be willing to come and help with the hospital. Paul prayed and sensed that this was something he should do. So he said yes.

That was twenty years ago. Today, Paul is an associate pastor and oversees the Lakewood Medical Mission Ministry outreach at our church. He performs life-saving surgeries in the bush country of Africa, on the earthquake-ravaged island of Haiti, in the war-torn country of Iraq—wherever God leads him. Because Paul was obedient to God's calling, God blessed him with a double portion. He has given Paul the desires of his heart and mind. By combining his love of medicine with his ministry calling, Paul has reached thousands with the message of Jesus Christ's healing, hope, and love for a hurting world.

Paul could have retreated into fear, anxiety, or even depression at the unfolding circumstances of his life. Or he could have second-guessed himself and listened to the folks in Arkansas who told him he was making a mistake, that he should just sit tight. But Paul didn't listen to those voices. He persisted and listened to God's still, small voice until God's timing brought forth the full measure of his calling for Paul into the light.

Trust God. Let Him lead you. Jesus says, " 'My yoke is easy' " (Matthew 11:30). Do you believe that? Walk in faith and see how your circumstances change. Don't let fear have any area of your life!

6

FEAR AFFECTS YOUR HEALTH

———○———

*Today you are drawing near for battle against
your enemies: let not your heart faint. Do not fear
or panic or be in dread of them, for the LORD your
God is he who goes with you to fight for you against
your enemies, to give you the victory.*

DEUTERONOMY 20:3–4

Fear affects your health in various ways:
- Anxiety attacks
- Nightmares
- Headaches
- Rashes
- Digestive disorders
- Depression

- Anger issues
- High blood pressure

Fear Is an Emotion, Real or Imagined

Fear is an emotion caused by a real or imagined threat. It causes a change in brain and organ function and ultimately a change in behavior, such as running away, hiding, or freezing. Fear is a vital response to physical and emotional danger. If we didn't feel it, we couldn't protect ourselves from legitimate threats. But often we fear situations that are far from life-or-death, and we can get hung up for no valid reason. Traumas or bad experiences can trigger a fear response within us that's hard to overcome.

Prominent psychologists such as John B. Watson, Robert Plutchik, and Paul Ekman suggest that there are only six basic emotions: anger, disgust, fear, happiness, sadness, and surprise.[8]

The Psychology Solution website theorizes the existence of an "anxiety scale," where "worry and mild concern are at one end of the spectrum, progressing through anxiety, to fear and blind panic at the other."[9]

Worry and anxiety – A set of responses to an unknown, imprecise or ill defined threat; often anticipatory in nature and created by the imagination. It's more associated with the need to be prepared. Worry leads to feeling anxious.

Fear and panic – A set of responses to a known, precise, well defined threat, which can be real or vividly imagined. It's mainly about avoidance and escape. In its extreme form, fear becomes panic.

Anxiety/panic sequence: Worry—Anxiety—Fear—Panic[10]

So while these emotions can help us in many ways, they can also work against us, which is why God in His mercy has given us His Word to overcome them. Let's take a closer look at these negative, sometimes unproductive emotions.

Worry

Worrying can actually be useful in helping to find solutions to problems. However, worrying often centers on problems that can't currently be solved. Worrisome thinking can easily become negative and doom-laden, making us feel anxious, helpless, overloaded, conflicted, and uncertain over how to handle a situation.

Anxiety

You're driving along a highway, expecting a crash is going to happen at any minute. What if you run into another car? What if someone runs into you? What if something falls out the back of that truck and hits your windshield? What if the tires blow? You become tense, jumpy, on edge. You scream at anyone or anything that feels like a potential threat.

Anxiety is focusing on a stressful situation you can't control. It's an attempt to stay safe, a survival tactic. This approach serves us well when we're faced with a real threat. But this thinking leads to many unresolved what-ifs, and you settle on the most catastrophic outcome.

Trying to deal with potentially disastrous scenarios at work or home often leads to feeling apprehensive and fearful. But with a little planning and faith, the outcome can be a blessing.

Fear

Fear in the natural world puts your body in a state of readiness so your mind can quickly step into action if something bad happens. A threat of something dangerous, or at least unpleasant, is sensed. The intensity of the fear depends on how serious the threat. If the object of fear is imagined vividly, physical changes may occur in the body, such as rapid breathing to take in more oxygen, a raised heartbeat to pump oxygen-rich blood to your muscles that have been supercharged with adrenaline, or sweating to cool the body and give your hands a better grip.

A high level of fear will cause the adrenal glands to produce a hormone that allows you to flee quickly if there is real danger. But if your body is constantly dealing with stresses that aren't actually dangerous, your adrenals will become depleted, which can seriously damage your body.

Imagine yourself standing on a high platform over a pool. You want to dive in. After all, you climbed all the way up there. But now you're thinking, *What if I die when I hit the water?* Fear gets the better of your enthusiasm and drains your courage. You consider running back down the ladder. But your friends are egging you on, cheering for your success. Eventually, you either give in to fear and come down to solid ground or you overcome that fear, let out a scream, and jump in.

Over and over Scripture tells us, "Do not fear," "Be not afraid," and "Be not fearful." In response, we worry about how to not live in fear. All we really need to do is turn toward God and rely on his love, because his perfect love casts out all fear (1 John 4:18).

Panic

Panic is an extreme form of fear. It happens when you are faced with sudden, life-threatening danger. The panic response prepares the body for survival by getting ready to fight or flee or freeze.

Panic attacks can happen even when there is no truly dangerous situation. You experience a fast-beating heart, clammy palms, a tight chest, shortness of breath, and dizziness. Your adrenaline is pumping. Your body is using a lot of energy preparing to get out of danger—even though you're perfectly safe.

Anger

Anger is fear on adrenaline. When you're afraid and you don't want to be, you mask it by being aggressive.

Anger makes us feel strong and in control. But fear is often the reason behind anger. Whenever you find yourself feeling angry, ask yourself, *What am I afraid of?*

If you shout at other drivers, you might be afraid they could damage your car or make you late for an appointment. If you're angry at someone who made fun of you, you might be afraid of what others might think about you if you didn't stand up for yourself.

Anger management involves techniques such as controlling your breath and counting from one to ten. But unless you understand the fear behind your anger, such techniques will not work effectively. To control anger, you must learn how to control your fears.

So if someone starts shouting at you, try to consider the reasons that might be behind their anger so you can comfort their fears. Of course, if someone is violently using anger against you, get away as quickly and safely as you can. Anger is justified aggression to defeat a perceived threat. But when you use anger to mask your fear and vulnerability, it becomes unproductive and can escalate into violence.

One day, as I was walking my dogs near my home, an older couple with their dog came down the street toward me. The man was acting very agitated, and his dog started growling at my dogs. My dogs, wanting to protect me, snarled back. One of my dogs somehow broke free from its collar. The man, thinking his smaller dog was in danger, kicked my dog. My other dog came to the first one's aid. As I tried to get my dog back on the leash, the man started yelling and cursing.

His wife calmly told him, "Just pick up your dog." When he attempted that, he got entangled in the leashes.

If someone were watching from a distance, the scene probably looked ridiculous. But this man's fear made the situation chaotic.

I got my dogs under control and apologized. When the man calmed down a bit, he explained that another dog had attacked a dog he'd owned and had killed it. Once I realized his fear, I told him I understood and was sorry for his loss. He apologized for losing control.

If I had yelled back at him, it would have been like pouring gas on a flame. Instead I learned a valuable lesson about working from a place of love and charity rather than fear and aggression.

Anger is sometimes caused by fear. Knowing this and controlling your fears can help manage your anger more effectively.

Depression

Depression can be a result of chemical imbalances in the brain. Constant anxiety, anger, and fear alter the good-feeling chemicals (serotonin, dopamine, and endorphins that maintain our mood balance and our brain's pleasure center) and eventually leave a person feeling overwhelmed and thinking that life is hopeless. These thoughts can be paralyzing or can lead a person to consider just ending it all.

Fear can attract more negative thoughts and actions. Fear even attracts more fear. Fear defeats you. It discourages you from acting in a positive way, and it brings despair and musters anger.

If you squeeze yourself into certain situations and behaviors that are not faith filled, godly, and upright, your fear will become evident. It surfaces through anxiety, depression, and anger. It denies you joy because you are fearful that something bad is going to happen even when nothing is threatening you at that moment.

When we are under a lot of pressure, we can become fearful. We try to control our situation, making sure everything gets done, dotting every *i* and crossing every *t*. In spite of our best efforts, things go wrong. If that happens often enough, we see our lives as being totally outside our control, which can lead to feelings of depression.

The best way to deal with stressful circumstances is to "let go and let God." When we realize that God has everything under control, our anxiety subsides, fear turns to peace, and depression dissipates. The devil wants to make us fear filled so we don't do what we are supposed to do. As long as he has us on a treadmill of fear and depression, we'll just keep running in place, never getting anywhere.

Don't believe the enemy. Take charge of your thoughts, as 2 Corinthians 10:3–6 says:

> Though we walk in the flesh, we are not waging war according to the flesh. For the weapons of our warfare are not of the flesh but have divine power to destroy strongholds. We destroy arguments and every lofty

opinion raised against the knowledge of God, and take every thought captive to obey Christ, being ready to punish every disobedience, when your obedience is complete.

Insecurity

There is another emotion that creeps in and steals your authority. All of us have at some point felt like we don't measure up. Somebody once told you that you weren't pretty enough, or smart enough, or talented enough, and you thought, *They must know something I don't.* Whenever you have to step out and do something, that little voice inside you nags and convinces you, *Don't even try.*

Our Lord and Savior doesn't feel that way about you. He died because you were precious to Him. Why think any less of yourself than your Creator does?

Proverbs 31:30 says beauty is fleeting (NIV) and vain. And not even the most beautiful models think they are perfect. So many successful people were told at one point or another, "You don't have what it takes," but they went on to win high recognition and awards. You can't go by what other people think, or even what you think of yourself, if it's not grounded in truth.

God is not a respecter of position or fame; He sees you for the perfect creation He made. He sees us as children made of light. He wants you to walk in confidence. He wants you to know that with Him you can accomplish all you set out to do. You have to understand who you are and whose you are to fully manifest your God-given gifts.

He wants you
to know that
with Him you can
accomplish all
things you set out
to do!

One day Jesus was walking through a massive crowd, with people pressing in from all sides. A woman who'd been suffering with a blood disease for twelve years had spent all her money on physicians but no one could heal her. She came up behind Jesus and touched the fringe of his garment, and immediately her discharge ceased.

Jesus asked, "Who was it that touched me?"

When everyone denied it, Peter said, "Master, the crowds surround you and are pressing in on you!"

But Jesus said, "Someone touched me, for I perceive that power has gone out from me."

When the woman realized that she had not been hidden after all, she came forward, trembling, and fell down before Jesus. She declared in the presence of all the people why she had touched him and how she had been immediately healed. Jesus said to her, "Daughter, your faith has made you well; go in peace" (see Luke 8:43–48).

She didn't accept the reports that the doctors had given her. She believed that her faith would make her whole. She knew who He was and who she was in Him. She knew who Jesus was and what He could do for her.

The man I consider a spiritual godfather, Pastor John Osteen, used to say, "How big is your *want-to*?" He was referring to faith. The woman in this parable had faith. Her "want-to" was more than enough. She tapped into God's power and was instantly healed.

What is your heart's desire? And how well does your faith stand up to fear, doubt, and insecurity?

Jeremiah 29:12–14 says, "You will call upon me and come and pray to me, and I will hear you. You will seek me and find me, when you seek me with all your heart. I will be found by you, declares the LORD." Jeremiah 30:17 says, "I will restore health to you, and your wounds I will heal, declares the LORD."

God is not hiding from you. He is available to answer your call, to take care of you, to heal you and mend you.

7

FAITH BRINGS FREEDOM

—————○—————

When one turns to the Lord, the veil is removed.
Now the Lord is the Spirit, and where the Spirit
of the Lord is, there is freedom.

2 CORINTHIANS 3:16–17

God has promised you deliverance from the shackles of fear. Psalm 34:4 tells us, "I sought the Lord, and he answered me and delivered me from all my fears." You don't need to be afraid. Jesus tells us in John 14:27, "'Peace I leave with you; my peace I give to you. Not as the world gives do I give to you. Let not your hearts be troubled, neither let them be afraid.'"

Faith frees you to soar, to be confident, to achieve, to conquer, to live undaunted, to be at peace and filled with joy.

Truth Sets You Free

In John 8:31–36, Jesus told his followers, "'If you abide in My word, you are My disciples indeed. And you shall know the truth, and the truth shall make you free.' They answered Him, 'We … have never been in bondage to anyone. How can you say, "You will be made free?" ' Jesus answered them, '… whoever commits sin is a slave to sin. And a slave does not abide in the house forever, but a son abides forever. Therefore if the Son makes you free, you shall be free indeed'" (NKJV).

If you are a slave to sin, you cannot use the power of Christ effectively because it can't abide in you. Fear is not believing, not putting your faith in God's promises. So when you are acting on fear instead of faith, you are sinning against God's authority.

God has given you a spirit of faith. If you are living in fear, anxiety, and depression, you are rejecting the very nature that God has given you. By accepting defeat because of your fear, you are rejecting Jesus' death, His sacrifice, so you can live.

By affirming your faith every day, you can resist fear, push back anger, and heal depression. This realization is the true power of faith in the face of fear.

Your relationship with God is the foundation on which to build your dreams, your successes, and your accomplishments. Nothing is impossible with God if you are connected to his supernatural power through faith. Then, what you see yourself believing in and doing, you can manifest into being.

The truth is, you are a child of God, and with Him all things are possible, if you believe.

Psalm 46:1–2 says, "God is our refuge and strength, an ever-present help in trouble. Therefore we will not fear, though the earth give way" (NIV). Be confident. God's outcome will be successful. When you are self-assured in your faith, you are free and not bound. You can dream as big as you want.

God can't work through you if you feel condemned, if you're afraid to follow His voice. Repent of that idea. He wants to use you now. He says, "I have something for you to do!"

This is where you have to be bold:

- Ask for forgiveness and move forward.
- Don't stay stuck in condemnation.
- Don't get captured by your thoughts.
- Don't let the enemy ruin you.
- Don't believe the lie that God has forsaken you.

God's mercy is never-ending. It covers you and it forgives you until you are reunited with Him in spirit. The only one who can turn away is you. If you turn your back on Christ, then you will surely die. Your anointing is in the Spirit, and living as His child you are assured everlasting life.

Therefore, as the apostle Paul says in Colossians 1:9–11, do not cease praying, "asking that you may be filled with the knowledge of his will in all spiritual wisdom and understanding, so as to walk in a manner worthy of the Lord, fully pleasing to him: bearing fruit in every good work and increasing in the knowledge of God; being strengthened with all power, according to his glorious might."

When you set out to do something, you don't expect it to turn out badly. You strive to accomplish good and successful works. However, if you are not seeking God's wisdom along the way, those plans may not come to fruition. Only when you set the plans before God and ask Him to provide you with the path, will things come to pass that you may not have even thought of.

Second Corinthians 9:8 says, "God is able to make all grace abound to you, so that having all sufficiency in all things at all times, you may abound in every good work." With God, all our needs are met.

When I started working on my Generation Hope Project ministry, I was confident that I could gather together the volunteers for our first event in the nation's capital. God had equipped me with the knowledge of how that city was run, and He had blessed me with friends and colleagues who could help me work with local partners to bring attention to various charities and organizations that needed help and volunteers. God brought things together as volunteers came from all over the world. Local churches and elected leaders agreed to become community partners so that after the Generation Hope Project was finished, the substantive changes we had initiated would continue.

One resident who participated in that day's efforts had seen his share of bad luck. But he said, "After seeing what this group has done for us in this community, I know there is a

God!" My partners and I were on cloud nine, happy to have been a blessing and to see so many people come to know the Lord and renew their relationships with Him. God had given us a magnificent gift, and we could rest in the knowledge that we had been faithful.

As I flew home, it dawned on me that we were going to have to do this all over again next year, in a different city with other officials and community partners. I laid my head on the seat tray and prayed, *God, show me what to do!* He answered, "Don't worry. I've got you in my hands." I raised my head. *Okay. But what's the plan?* He replied, "All in due time." I confirmed, *Well, okay then, Lord. This is all you.*

My feelings went from cold realization to quiet trust.

From that moment on, I relied on Him for our partners and volunteers. I didn't worry about the outcome of any events we organized. And in each city we have served, God's favor preceded us and supernaturally opened doors. God manifested His will in my life and the lives of our participants.

Because of the faith we stand on, the hope of things not yet seen, God has made the Generation Hope Project a success for all who participate. Year after year, for six years now, He has manifested a miraculous movement of hope and ministry to communities across the country. He is faithful to His call on this ministry.

My director of logistics is an awesome man of God and a true friend. I rely on him to get the materials and serve meals to the volunteers in an organized and efficient way. This year, he told us he could not break away from work to join us.

Though this news might have caused me to worry, I knew God would provide. I prayed for God to bring me someone who could get the job done.

For weeks, no one seemed to be available. A few names came up, but no one was quite right. Then when I went to Austin for my nephew's graduation, I started talking with one of the Generation Hope Project volunteers who was also attending, and I mentioned that we needed a replacement logistics director.

God put it on my heart to ask him if he would be interested in the job. As we talked, I realized that he was the perfect fit. And we both thought of someone who could assist him with the duties, another young man who had volunteered with us before and who was also graduating that day. Instantly I had an awesome team ordained by God. To His glory, my problem was solved—with a double portion.

There is no greater peace than when you leave your problems in God's hands. That doesn't mean you don't have to do the work. But if you listen to what God is saying to you and go where He leads you, He will bring the perfect resources across your path.

God is a restorer and a provider of power to your faith. Through tireless faith and hope, the seemingly impossible will come to pass and the improbable things are changed. These testimonies of faith in action let you know just how ready God is to work through you, to show His love for His children.

At our last Generation Hope Project event in Detroit, a

young woman who had breathing difficulties signed up to work with us. She had been hooked up to an oxygen machine for more than a year, but she believed that she would be off the machine by the time we went to Detroit. She registered in the fall 2015 to serve with us in summer 2016. As the date approached, she went to see her doctor in the hope that he would tell her she was well enough to travel. Two weeks before the event, her doctor took her off the oxygen tank, affirming she was healed! Her faith made her whole.

This woman was a tremendous help to us with registration since she was familiar with the computer program we were using, and she worked tirelessly at the food bank, sorting produce. She said, "I have heard Pastor Joel say, 'While you are waiting for a miracle, become a miracle for someone else.' Well, I have experienced the miracles of God, and Generation Hope was an opportunity for God to use me to serve others."

What a testament! Faith can change your heart and renew your spirit, sometimes in the most unlikely situations.

In one city, a woman shared with us that her husband, who was with her to serve, wasn't a practicing Christian. She had been praying for many years that God would soften his heart. We prayed over her and asked God to move her husband through his volunteering experience.

After the last day, I asked them what their most impactful moment was. She said, "Having my husband serving with me." He said he was grateful for what he and his wife had and that he realized the great need of others.

Later, this woman texted me: *My husband just told me that this is the first time in his 58 years of life that he has ever given back ... and he has never felt so good. He said, 'Now I know why you do service work.' Thank you!* God is faithful to answer our prayers.

Not long ago, we served in San Francisco's City Impact Church neighborhood, delivering meals to the public-housing residents. Two of our volunteers, Ester and Patricia, went out knocking on doors. At one building known for sex trafficking, a young woman opened the door. Before she said a word, Ester broke into tears and was unable to speak, though she wasn't sure why. Ester had never met this young woman and didn't know her story. The Holy Spirit filled them, and the young woman started to cry. Ester and Patricia offered to pray with her and asked if she wanted to pray for something. The young woman asked them to pray for her son who had been taken away from her. She hadn't seen him in some time.

They prayed the blood of Jesus over her and her son. They asked the Lord to plant the seed of righteousness within her and guide her to the path He had for her so she could be the mother she was supposed to be. They prayed for God to strengthen her household and show her the life of abundance that was waiting for her as a born-again believer. After they finished praying, Ester and Patricia offered her one of the lunches they had brought and told her God loves her.

The faith of those volunteers allowed them to reach into people's lives that day. God knows the end from the beginning, and He works all things together for good.

By affirming your faith every day, you can resist fear, push back anger, and heal depression.

God's knowledge of each of our needs is so complete. He uses each one of us at whatever place we are in our walk. He can use you to be a blessing too. He wants to use you to change circumstances, to do great and mighty things even through the most mundane of activities. He weaves a tapestry from the finest threads and the plainest of threads, and it all comes together through great and mighty works of faith. We are the majesty of His creation with the beauty of His image in each of us and all for His glory and praise.

8

FAITH PRODUCES JOY

---○---

*The fruit of the Spirit is love, joy, peace, forbearance,
kindness, goodness, faithfulness, gentleness and self-control.*

GALATIANS 5:22–23 NIV

John 15:11 says, "'These things I have spoken to you, that my joy may be in you, and that your joy may be full.'" Operating in faith brings a joy and contentment that will see you through every day. The kind of faith that creates relationship with God the Father, his Son Jesus Christ, and the Holy Spirit is a consuming fire that produces a shining, Spirit-filled joy.

God gives us an unspeakable, overflowing joy that keeps us going through the trials of life in spite of hardship. The world doesn't understand this joy. But when you have the fullness of faith and love, you truly have something to be joyful about.

Habakkuk 3:18 says, "I will rejoice in the LORD; I will take joy in the God of my salvation." And Psalm 35:9 says, "My soul shall be joyful in the LORD: it shall rejoice in his salvation" (KJV). Psalm 100:4 says, "Enter his gates with thanksgiving, and his courts with praise! Give thanks to him; bless his name!"

Acts 13:52 says, "The disciples were filled with joy and with the Holy Spirit." And Acts 2:28 says, "You have made known to me the paths of life; you will make me full of gladness with your presence." In *Strong's Concordance*, the Greek word for *joy* is *euphrosuné*, which means "joy, gladness, rejoicing."[11] Exuberant joy produces strength, and in God's strength, we can face anything.

Isaiah 61:7 says, "They will possess a double portion. ... Everlasting joy will be theirs" (NASB). The Hebrew word for *joy* in *Strong's Concordance* is *simchah*, meaning "exceeding joy, celebration, to delight in and be joyful."[12]

Isaiah 61:10 says, "I will greatly rejoice in the LORD, my soul shall be joyful in my God; for he hath clothed me with the garments of salvation, he hath covered me with the robe of righteousness, as a bridegroom decketh himself with ornaments, and as a bride adorneth herself with her jewels" (KJV). Isaiah 61:11 says, "As the earth bursts with spring wildflowers, and as a garden cascades with blossoms, so the Master, GOD, brings righteousness into full bloom and puts praise on display before the nations" (MSG).

Your strength comes from the Lord, and your joy comes from Him. When you raise your voice in praise and worship, you will feel the victory in your core.

Isaiah 61:3 says God will give us "a crown of beauty for ashes, a joyous blessing instead of mourning, festive praise instead of despair" (NLT). Jesus, the author of your faith, cannot be shaken. Let God give you grace to accept your calling, then operate in that faith and authority.

To Know Joy Is to Know God

Joy is what you feel on your wedding day, or when you gaze into your newborn's eyes. It's in a child's squeals of delight at sledding down a hill of fluffy snow. Joy comes from achieving a great accomplishment that you have strived to complete. But it comes most easily and powerfully when you have a sustaining relationship with God, when you believe in His Word, and when you put your trust and faith in Him.

To know God's love for you is to be filled with joy—to go about confident, without doubt, and in total peace. The Bible calls it rejoicing. Joy is a fruit of the Spirit, according to Galatians 5:23.

Nehemiah 8:10 says, "'Do not be grieved, for the joy of the LORD is your strength.'" Faith is the victory that overcomes the world, and the joy of the Lord is what sustains you.

Romans 15:13 says, "May the God of hope fill you with all joy and peace in believing, so that by the power of the Holy Spirit you may abound in hope."

God's love
is personal.
He knows each
of us individually.

Faith, Hope, and Trust

In 1 Corinthians 13:13, faith is listed as one of three virtues that we can attain; the other two are hope and love (agape love). Each of these virtues leads to the next, and each supports the others. Love is the greatest of the gifts because love connects us to God, and God is love.

Faith is the hope of what you are assured: that you will dwell with God for eternity because He loves you.

God wants us to love Him with our whole hearts and our whole minds. And yet we don't. He told us to have no other gods above him (Exodus 20:3), and yet we do. He commanded us to love one another as we love ourselves, and we can't do it. No wonder we cower in fear. If we avoid building a relationship with our Creator, we will find it difficult to put our trust in Him.

When God made Adam and Eve, He told them to avoid the fruit of the tree of good and evil. They had just one commandment, and they couldn't keep it.

I have often wondered why Adam and Eve sinned against God. He had supplied everything they would ever need, including eternal life. Would you have turned away from what God asked of Adam and Eve? Like teenagers who think they're smarter than their parents, Adam and Eve believed they could figure it out on their own. They turned away from their Creator and put their trust in themselves.

Yet that's exactly what we do when we act in fear instead of faith, when we rely on ourselves and act on the knowledge of good and evil rather than trusting in God's goodness and believing that He will provide for us.

To Know God Is to Know Love

God's being is light. His essence is love. His Word is our salvation.

God's love is personal. He knows each of us individually. His mighty love has no beginning and no end. The Greek word *agape* is often translated as "love" in the New Testament. The essence of agape love is goodwill, benevolence, and delight in the object of love.

This experiencing of God's love defines you as His child. Your natural spiritual state is to abide in His love. When His creation sinned, we were redeemed because of His great love for us. As earthly creatures, our souls long to be with Him again as we struggle within this bodily form that contains us.

When we fill up on God's hope, His joy resides in us. Have you ever considered the joy Jesus must feel when He looks at you, His creation, and sees you awakened to the purpose for your life?

Through Jesus Christ and His redemption, we know that He exists and we can discern the nature of His being. We believe in His mercy, kindness, and love for us. Our redemption comes from relying on Him.

Your faith is made enduring by His love. Ephesians 3:17–19 says that "Christ may dwell in your hearts through faith—that you, being rooted and grounded in love, may have strength to comprehend with all the saints what is the breadth and length and height and depth, and to know the love of Jesus Christ that surpasses knowledge, that you may be filled with all the fullness of God."

Deuteronomy 31:6 says, "Be strong and courageous. Do not be afraid or terrified because of [our enemies], for the LORD your God goes with you; he will never leave you nor forsake you" (NIV).

Second Corinthians 6:16 says, "We are the temple of the living God; as God said, 'I will make my dwelling among them and walk among them, and I will be their God, and they shall be my people.'"

To Know God Is to Know His Power and Authority

So up to this point we have been talking a lot about faith in God, but what about the power of His Word and about His faithfulness to you.

Consider the power God has given you through faith to fight off fear. If we understand what that power in us can do, and what we can achieve by believing in Jesus' promise to give us this power and authority, then we will be able to achieve anything in line with His will.

In Matthew 16:18, Jesus told Peter, "I will build my church, and the gates of hell shall not prevail against it." Jesus is building His church through each and every one who believes in Him.

In Ephesians 1:17–21, the apostle Paul tells us about the power and authority of Jesus. Then Paul asks God to reveal to us "the Spirit of wisdom and of revelation in the knowledge of him, having the eyes of your hearts enlightened, that you may know what is the hope to which he has called you, what are the riches of his glorious inheritance in the saints, and what is the immeasurable greatness of his power toward us who believe, according to the working of his great might that he worked in Christ when he raised him from the dead and seated him at his right hand in the heavenly places, far above all rule and authority and power and dominion, and above every name that is named, not only in this age but also in the one to come."

So what's keeping that holy power from being fully realized in your life? The answer is simple. You can't use God's authority if you're not living under that authority.

In John 5:30, Jesus told the people, "I pass no judgment without consulting the Father. I judge as I am told. And my judgment is absolutely fair and just, for it is according to the will of God who sent me and is not merely my own" (TLB).

You may ask, "If I have the same power as Jesus, why can't I get healed or fight off the enemy?" Hosea 4:6 says, "My people are destroyed for lack of knowledge." If we have no knowledge or understanding of God's true Word, then how can we call on it with authority?

You can call on Jesus' authority for deliverance and healing, just as He did when He called on his God-given right and proved both His faith in God the Father and His faith in the authority given to Him.

Your God-given authority is an absolute power handed to you by Jesus Christ. But using that power is relative to the decisions you make and your abilities. If you are in agreement with God, and His purpose and your faith are aligned, your power in the Holy Spirit will be strong. And when the enemy tries to compromise the power of God in you through fear, unbelief, rebellion, and other sinful thoughts and emotions, your faith will be a shield and God's light will prevail against the enemy.

Matthew 18:18–20 says, "'Assuredly, I say to you, whatever you bind on earth will be bound in heaven, and whatever you loose on earth will be loosed in heaven. Again I say to you that if two of you agree on earth concerning anything that they ask, it will be done for them by My Father in heaven. For where two or three are gathered together in My name, I am there in the midst of them'" (NKJV).

When Jesus died and rose from the dead, He claimed His authority, and then He gave it back to us.

Order of Melchizedek

Hebrews 4:15–16 says, "We do not have a high priest who is unable to sympathize with our weaknesses, but one who in every respect has been tempted as we are, yet without sin. Let us then with confidence draw near to the throne of grace, that we may receive mercy and find grace to help in time of need."

Psalm 110:4 says Jesus was a priest "in the order of Melchizedek" (NLT). According to Hebrews 7:1, 3, Melchizedek was a "priest of the Most High God … without father or mother or genealogy." He brought bread and wine to bless Abraham, and Abraham gave him a tenth of all he had. In the online Encyclopedia Britannica, Melchizedek (which means "king of righteousness") was a king from Salem (which means "peace").[13] So he was the king of righteousness and peace, and he, according to Scripture, continues to live as a priest forever.

Who other than Jesus could be that king and high priest for us?

Everything you need to grow your faith is in the Bible. So read and study everything God has put into that book. His knowledge is at our disposal, His power is within us, and His salvation assures of everlasting life.

9

FAITH CALLS YOU TO ACTION

---○---

Trust in the LORD with all your heart, and do not lean on your own understanding. In all your ways acknowledge him, and he will make straight your paths. Be not wise in your own eyes; fear the LORD, and turn away from evil. It will be healing to your flesh and refreshment to your bones.

PROVERBS 3:5–8

Faith in Jesus Christ gives you the freedom to act on what He has put in your heart and in your dreams, and to act on the opportunities with which God blesses you. Faith also allows you to boldly take action from a solid foundation.

Ephesians 3:12 says we have "boldness and access with confidence" through our faith in Jesus. Luke 6:48 says those who come to Jesus, hear His words, and put them into practice are "like a man building a house, who dug deep and laid the foundation on the rock. And when the flood arose, the stream beat vehemently against that house, and could not shake it, for it was founded on the rock" (NKJV).

Matthew 14:14–21 tells of a powerful miracle Jesus performed:

> When he went ashore he saw a great crowd, and he had compassion on them and healed their sick. Now when it was evening, the disciples came to him and said, "This is a desolate place, and the day is now over; send the crowds away to go into the villages and buy food for themselves." But Jesus said, "They need not go away; you give them something to eat." They said to him, "We have only five loaves here and two fish." And he said, "Bring them here to me." Then he ordered the crowds to sit down on the grass, and taking the five loaves and the two fish, he looked up to heaven and said a blessing. Then he broke the loaves and gave them to the disciples, and the disciples gave them to the crowds. And they all ate and were satisfied. And they took up twelve baskets full of the broken pieces left over. And those who ate were about five thousand men, besides women and children.

The crowds sought Jesus for his wisdom and compassion, and so should we, in daily prayer and praise. He will then multiply our resources, our gifts, and our confidence in Him.

You may be thinking, *But Jesus had supernatural powers. Something like that could never happen today.* Well, let me tell you about something that did happened in Houston, Texas. One Tuesday night in June 2001, Lakewood Church (known as the Oasis of Love) was having a singles class meeting upstairs as usual, and the couples' fellowship was having a vows renewal ceremony in the sanctuary. The couples came dressed in formal attire, with some ladies even wearing their wedding gowns. They brought in catered food for three hundred people, with formal china and crystal adorning the tables.

As the excited couples started arriving, rain began coming down. Now, scattered showers and thunderstorms that come and go in a matter of hours are common in Houston. But this rainfall was different. It was the beginning of Tropical Storm Allison, which in 2001 devastated the region for six days, overwhelming the bayous and creeks and flooding low-lying areas.

Most freeways in the area became impassable, stranding motorists. Sections of downtown Houston lay under several feet of water. The midtown medical center had to evacuate many patients. Basements were inundated, and the water shorted out the vast computer mainframes that were kept there. The city had trouble getting first responders to people in need, and emergency patients had to be driven to facilities in other areas. Houston received more than thirty-five inches of rain in one week, making Allison the worst tropical storm in history.

As the rain got worse, that small group of churchgoers got stranded away from their homes. Excitement turned to concern as the reports of severe flooding turned their dream of creating lasting memories into a nightmare.

All around the church, homes were being destroyed by the rising water, but the church and its adjoining buildings were a dry oasis amid a sea of water. Neighborhood residents whose homes were waist deep in water came to the church seeking shelter. Suddenly the catered food that had been brought in for the festivities was feeding more than just the stranded group of churchgoers. The food was now going to feed all those who had sought shelter that night and the next day.

Babies and young children with their mothers, the elderly, and the infirm and disabled made their way to the dry building. The people who were arriving were drenched, and many carried their most valuable possessions with them in shopping bags. Many required medical attention because of their conditions.

In the days that followed, my husband and some of the other church leaders ventured out in SUVs to get supplies for the church, as more and more people arrived in rescue vehicles, dump trucks, and anything that could make it through the flood waters. As the local and national media reported on what was occurring at the church, citizens from far and wide braved the flood waters, bringing food and supplies, diapers, clothes, blankets, and fresh water. The church became a distribution center for those in need until the flood waters subsided. Lakewood Church became an unofficial emergency center for the area, ultimately sheltering an estimated three thousand flood victims.

What those church-going believers had intended to be a celebration turned into a rescue mission. And Houstonians came to realize what an oasis of love in a troubled world really meant. It was a supernatural faith manifestation of multiplying supply and rescue under the power of God's authority. It was a modern-day miracle and an example of God's love on display in human form.

And those people who hosted the fellowship events at the church will never forget what a few people can do for many if they let faith and God-given authority translate into full-fledged action.

That miracle happened because of unwavering faith and intercession.

Gird for Battle

Even if you have great faith, that doesn't mean you will never have trials or tribulations. The enemy is not going to surrender just because you declare victory. But you can withstand anything if you prepare well for the battles ahead.

Ephesians 3:17–21 says that Christ will "dwell in your hearts through faith—that you, being rooted and grounded in love ... may be filled with all the fullness of God. Now to him who is able to do far more abundantly than all that we ask or think, according to the power at work within us, to him be glory in the church and in Christ Jesus throughout all generations, forever and ever. Amen."

The Bible contains many examples of how men and women were able to withstand hardships through faith. In the book of Job, two chapters of great faith are followed by thirty-five chapters of questioning why suffering happened.

David wrestled with questions for years, especially while hiding from Saul and wondering if he'd live to see the reign the prophet had said would be his. He began his Psalm 13 with, "How long, O Lord? Will you forget me forever? How long will you hide your face from me?"

Mary and Martha cried out to God for their brother to be saved before he died. In John 11:21–22, Martha said to Jesus, " 'Lord, if you had been here, my brother would not have died. But even now I know that whatever you ask from God, God will give you.' " Then in verse 23, "Jesus said to her, 'Your brother will rise again.' " But ultimately, because these sisters believed in Jesus, they saw Lazarus' resurrected body come out of the grave.

The apostle Paul was stuck in a prison cell in Caesarea for two years. He learned that even when we don't know what to say to God in our despair, the Holy Spirit will pray on our behalf. Romans 8:26–27 says, "We do not know what we ought to pray for, but the Spirit himself intercedes for us" with words and utterances too deep for us to comprehend. "And he who searches our hearts knows the mind of the Spirit, because the Spirit intercedes for God's people in accordance with the will of God" (NIV).

You can't be
a candle in the
wind. You have to
be a lighthouse—
so full of light and
love that you
dispel all fear
and darkness.

God Creates with Light

So we know that God creates with light, His Word is our redeemer, His essence is love, and His power is almighty. I want you to think about this and really get it deep down in your spirit—because if you didn't know this already, it will serve to completely change your thinking.

When you are in a room filled with light, and next to it is a room filled with darkness, when you open the doors, darkness doesn't come into the lighted room and obscure the light. Of course not. The light in that room lights the other room and dispels the darkness.

Just think about that: light fills in everything. And because He is light, God resides in you and through you and around you! His power, His energy, His light is completely available to you.

God has given you His power to quell the darkness, to cast out fear with the power of faith, to live in a "yes, I can do all things" world. But you must prepare. You can't be a candle in the wind; you need to be a lighthouse—so full of light and love that you dispel all fear and darkness.

So what can you do? It's really easy to identify the things you need to do, but it takes everything to believe you can do them!

Grow Your Faith

To grow your faith, you need to strengthen the Word of God inside yourself. Ask God for direction. And seek Him diligently. Then every time fear or doubt comes into your head, ask yourself these questions:

- Why am I afraid?
- Why am I feeling unloved?
- Why am I hesitating?
- Why am I anxious?
- Why am I angry?
- Why do I not believe in myself?
- Why do I not believe I can defeat this situation?

You have to search deep inside your heart and be honest with yourself in order to find the answers. Where is your faith anchored? Is it nicely tucked in the highlighted pages of your Bible sitting on the shelf? Or do you carry it with you to draw upon and wield like a mighty sword against darkness and fear?

Here are some thoughts to replace those questions of fear with answers of faith:

- "There is no fear in love, but perfect love casts out fear" (1 John 4:18).
- "Without faith it is impossible to please him … [but] he rewards those who seek him" (Hebrews 11:6).
- "Do not be anxious about anything. … God will supply every need of yours according to his riches in glory in Christ Jesus" (Philippians 4:6, 19).
- "The LORD is merciful and gracious, slow to anger and abounding in steadfast love" (Psalm 103:8).

- "I can do all things through him who strengthens me" (Philippians 4:13).

As you become strong in your faith, God will use you to bring about good. Second Corinthians 4:5–7 says, "What we proclaim is not ourselves, but Jesus Christ as Lord, with ourselves as servants for Jesus' sake. For God, who said, 'Let light shine out of darkness,' has shone in our hearts to give the light of the knowledge of the glory of God in the face of Jesus Christ."

As you strengthen your faith, your words will produce fruit. You will speak victory, abundance, and blessings. The enemy will be powerless against you. But you have to stand strong, not wavering like a blade of grass in the breeze. Your words have to match your faith, your hope, and your trust. Claim the authority you have been given through Jesus!

Manifest Your Faith

Luke 17:20–21 says that when the Pharisees asked Jesus when the kingdom of God would come, he answered, "'The kingdom of God does not come by observation, nor will they say, "See here!" or "See there!" For indeed, the kingdom of God is in within you'" (NKJV).

So how can we manifest the kingdom of God within us?

To *manifest* means to be able to be seen, to show something clearly, and to understand or recognize something. So how do you manifest your faith? First John 4:7 says that we reveal the God within us through love: "Beloved, let us love one another, for love is from God, and whoever loves has been born of God and knows God."

Love is a core aspect of God's character, His person. God's love is not in conflict with His holiness, righteousness, justice, or even His wrath. All God's attributes are in perfect harmony. Everything God does is done in love, just as everything He does is just and right. God is the perfect example of true love.

Amazingly, God has given those who receive Jesus as their personal Savior the ability to love as He does, through the power of the Holy Spirit (see John 1:12; 1 John 3:1, 23–24).

First John 4:19 says that "because he first loved us" (NKJV) we can manifest His will through His love, and with His faith, power, and authority, call things as though they were. As believers, our words have power, and we need to begin to put them to work for us like God Himself does. The Bible tells us that He uses words "to calleth those things which be not as though they were" (Romans 4:17 KJV).

10

FAITH GIVES COMFORT

---○---

I have sent him to you for this very purpose,
that you may know how we are and that
he may encourage your hearts.

COLOSSIANS 4:8

Nothing brings more comfort than loving someone and knowing they truly love you back. First John 4:8 tells us that God is love. And he loves us with pure, unaltered love, the kind that can't entertain hate, the kind that overlooks our human faults, that rewards us.

Never was a more important declaration made than this: God is love. God doesn't just love; He is love. His nature and essence are love. Love permeates His very being. Because God's very nature is love, He wants to share His love, because doing so glorifies Him. Glorifying God is the highest and most noble act you can perform. He wants you to glorify Him because He is the highest and the best, and He deserves all glory.

God Is a Comforter

Faith is a substance that once you accept its power and might, it gives you comfort in knowing that you know that you know. God is a faithful God who is in a relationship with you to bring about good in your life and to give you peace as you do what He has called and enabled you to do.

God tells us in Isaiah 51:12, "'I am he who comforts you; who are you that you are afraid of man who dies, of the son of man who is made like grass?'" We don't need to fear man, because as eternal beings we can look beyond this earthly realm and use the strength God has given us, His spiritual descendants.

Second Corinthians 1:4 says He "comforts us in all our affliction, so that we may be able to comfort those who are in any affliction, with the comfort with which we ourselves are comforted by God." God wants to bless you, but He also wants you to be a blessing to others. Like His, our hearts can speak "out of the abundance of the heart" (Luke 6:45).

God is with us always. He tells us all the ways He walks with us in Psalm 23:

- When we are in need: "The LORD is my shepherd; I shall not want" (v. 1).
- When we need to rest: "He makes me lie down in green pastures" (v. 2).

- When we are thirsty: "He leads me beside still waters" (v. 2).
- When our emotions and thoughts are out of control: "He restores my soul" (v. 3).
- When we are trying to find our way: "He leads me in the paths of righteousness for his name's sake" (v. 3).
- When things look uncertain: "Even though I walk through the valley of the shadow of death, I will fear no evil, for you are with me" (v. 4).
- When we need protection: "Your rod and Your staff, they comfort me" (v. 4).
- When we are hungry: "You prepare a table before me in the presence of my enemies" (v. 5).
- When we need healing: "You anoint my head with oil" (v. 5).
- When we need to be filled up in our spirits: "My cup overflows" (v. 5).
- Wherever we go, until the end of our lives: "Surely goodness and mercy shall follow me all the days of my life, and I shall dwell in the house of the Lord forever" (v. 6).

He is more than enough, our El Shaddai, the finisher of our faith, the lover of our souls. Of what shall we be afraid?

Faith Is Like Bread

If you have ever made bread from scratch, you know it takes a long time from the time you decide to make it to the moment

He is always there, available and willing to forgive you so that you can be in a true, loving relationship with Him.

when you taste that warm slice of bread covered with melting butter.

First you have to gather all the best ingredients—the best ground flour, warm artesian water, raw cane sugar, sea salt, and living yeast. Then you mix them all and form it into a ball. Knead the dough on a floured board. Then let it rise in a warm spot with a moist towel over it. Once it's risen, you knead it down again, work the dough, and let it rise a second time. Finally, you put it in a pan and stick it in the oven to bake. You can smell the goodness all through the house. Finally, you slice it, slather it with butter, and sink your teeth into that soft, delicious goodness.

Faith is like homemade bread. You have to use the best ingredients, and you have to work patiently to get the final product. And if you want to have faith every day, you have to make time to work on it every day. First Chronicles 16:11 says, "Seek the LORD and his strength; seek his presence continually!"

Have you ever made a new year's resolution to get healthy? You go through the fridge and pantry, throwing away all the fattening things. You go to the grocery store and buy yogurt, veggies, fruit, and lean meat. You go online and find all the juices and smoothies and paleo meals you can make. Then you join a gym or buy an exercise machine. You start working out and eating well all through January, determined to do this!

Then February comes, and you slip a little around Valentine's Day. By March, all that home equipment is layered with your workout clothes. Then comes spring break and thoughts of beaches and pool parties, and you get back into the routine. You learn that the more you work out with a goal in mind, the better you stick to it!

Faith is like a workout. To reach your goals, you have to be committed. Every day, whether you feel like it or not, you get into your workout clothes. You warm up and stretch, starting slowly with easy moves. Then you do reps until you feel the burn. Those extra pounds begin dropping off until you're left with lean muscle and a body that has stamina and strength.

Faith is like that too. You read the Bible every day, standing on the faith Scriptures. You move on to the praise and worship Scriptures. As you begin to understand the Spirit of the Lord, you learn to call on Him throughout the day. Eventually you develop a faith that can withstand the difficulties of life instead of giving in to them. You now have faith that has stamina and strength.

His Love Is Warm and Cozy

Have you ever felt God's love? Many people who have had near-death or out-of-body experiences say they have, and that they felt completely filled with joy.

I once had a unique experience that allowed me to feel God's love for me. I was coming home from work one day, and as I was almost to my house, a supernatural feeling hit me, unlike anything I'd felt before or since. The only way to describe it is that it felt like a big warm hug that got rid of all fear and anxiety. It made me feel completely at peace, completely whole. That warm and cozy sensation brought to life all the promises in Scripture about how much God loves me. I guess He thought I needed to realize it at that moment.

His love is not like that intoxicatingly romantic longing you feel for your spouse. It's not that proud, protective feeling you have for your kids. It's not even the approval-seeking kind of love you have for your parents. God's love is the pure emotion of a Creator for his creation. It is the reuniting of a human soul with the Holy Spirit. It's a feeling of completion, reuniting, true peace, and joy.

In Jeremiah 31:3, God tells us, "I have loved you with an everlasting love; therefore I have continued my faithfulness to you."

Faith will bring you to that place. If you seek Him, He will be as real to you as any being in this realm. God is not some elusive essence in a cloud that plays hide-and-seek with us. He is always there, available and willing to forgive you so that you can be in a true, loving relationship with Him.

Romans 4:20–21 says of Abraham, "No unbelief made him waver concerning the promise of God, but he grew strong in his faith as he gave glory to God, fully convinced that God was able to do what he had promised."

11

FAITH LEADS TO VICTORY

<hr>

*Thanks be to God, who gives us the victory through our
Lord Jesus Christ. Therefore, my beloved brothers, be
steadfast, immovable, always abounding in the work of the
Lord, knowing that in the Lord your labor is not in vain.*

1 CORINTHIANS 15:57–58

Galatians 6:8 says, "The one who sows to his own flesh will
from the flesh reap corruption, but the one who sows to
the Spirit will from the Spirit reap everlasting life."

That is the victory. Faith is the evidence and the substance *in you*. If you have this faith, then God has established
the victory in you. He has established the evidence of what
He intended to attain when He created you: your everlasting
salvation and a relationship of love with you for all eternity.

In order to obtain the victory, you have to break the habit of fear and establish the habit of faith.

Your Labor Is Not in Vain

To break a habit takes a lot more time than to acquire one. If you've developed a habit of saying, "I'm afraid. I can't do that," it needs to be broken; you need to stop repeating that. Change your confession!

Instead, proclaim that you are well able to accomplish all that God has set in your heart to do: "When I am afraid, I put my trust in you" (Psalm 56:3). Proverbs 18:10 says, "The name of the Lord is a strong tower; the righteous man runs into it and is safe."

Just as you need to discipline yourself to work out and take care of chores, you have to spend time in prayer and believe the promises of God. Listen to Him speak life into you. He is your partner, and with Him all things can be accomplished.

Like breathing, praying should come naturally. If you set aside time to be in His presence, He will be there all through the day to help you with your decisions and to lead you on the path that brings success. Your efforts will not be in vain.

Deuteronomy 28:8–14 says:

The Lord will command the blessing on you in your barns and in all that you undertake. And he will bless you in the land that the Lord your God is giving you. The Lord will establish you as a people holy to himself, as he has sworn to you, if you keep the commandments of the LORD your God and walk in his ways. And all the peoples of the earth shall see that you are called by the name of the LORD, and they shall be afraid of you. And the LORD will make you abound in prosperity, in the fruit of your womb and in the fruit of your livestock and in the fruit of your ground, within the land that the LORD swore to your fathers to give you. The LORD will open to you his good treasury, the heavens, to give the rain to your land in its season and to bless all the work of your hands. And you shall lend to many nations, but you shall not borrow. And the LORD will make you the head and not the tail, and you shall only go up and not down, if you obey the commandments of the LORD your God, which I command you today, being careful to do them, and if you do not turn aside from any of the words that I command you today, to the right hand or to the left, to go after other gods to serve them.

That's a mighty promise!

The Scripture goes on to tell about all the calamities that will come on us if we turn away, if we are disobedient, if we sin against God. But for now, let's concentrate on the blessings. Count all the ways He wants to make us successful in that passage. If you seek Him and obey His commands, He promises food, wealth, children, power, prestige, position, success, skilled hands, prosperity, and holy relationship. Wow!

God has laid out for us what it takes to get these promises. Are you leading the kind of life that puts Him first? The Word of God is a living spirit that dwells in us, and we have the power and authority to manifest all these blessings if we live in relationship with Him.

A Measure of Success

Faith allows us to succeed. But success is not measured in treasure alone.

Let's say you are going to church, giving tithes and offerings, praying every day, and blessing others. Your words are casting down fear, anger, anxiety, and depression. But then trouble comes along, and you fall into old habits of fear and worry. When that happens, you have to dust yourself off and get back on track. Seek out Scriptures that will fight off fear. Sometimes fasting and meditation are the only way to get out of your head and into the Spirit. And that's okay. Even Jesus sought out time alone with God when big things were happening in His life.

The measure of success for a life well lived is not the amount of stuff you bought and collected. It's not how well you danced or how many reps you could do in one workout. It's how you lived. Were you a blessing to people? Did you leave a legacy of love, service, and success for the next generation?

Second Corinthians 4:13 says, "Since we have the same spirit of faith according to what has been written, 'I believed, and so I spoke,' we also believe, and so we also speak." Gauge your success by how many lives you impact for good. If your actions inspire others to dream, to accomplish things they thought they couldn't do, to become better than they would have been otherwise, you will have led an accomplished and successful life.

Invest in other people. If you give of yourself with an open hand, if you assist others with no expectation of gain, the rewards will return to you many times over and to your children and their children to many generations.

Luke 1:50 says, "'His mercy is for those who fear him from generation to generation.'" Luke 6:38 says, "'Give, and it will be given to you. Good measure, pressed down, shaken together, running over, it will be put into your lap. For with the measure you use it will be measured back to you.'"

This love for one another—the Christ in each of us—that God will bless.

Standing on Faith

Sometimes we stand on the shoulders of our forefathers and foremothers who believed and prayed on our behalf. Sometimes its their sins that create generational curses, but we can be the ones to stop that problem from being passed on. When you pray in faith over your children or loved ones, God will protect and guide them, and they will thrive.

Isaiah 54:13–14 says, "All your children shall be taught by the LORD, and great shall be the peace of your children. In righteousness you shall be established; you shall be far from oppression, for you shall not fear; and from terror, for it shall not come near you."

Paul recognized generational blessings when he wrote 2 Timothy 1:5: "I am reminded of your sincere faith, a faith that dwelt first in your grandmother Lois and your mother Eunice and now, I am sure, dwells in you as well."

There is no greater inheritance you could leave to your children than a legacy of faith, hope, and love.

Numbers 14:18 says the Lord will visit "the iniquity of the fathers on the children, to the third and the fourth generation." But Isaiah 58:12 says, "You shall raise up the foundations of many generations; you shall be called the repairer of the breach." We can change our future generation's legacy if we follow God's will.

Children born to mothers during the Dutch famine at the end of World War II had susceptibilities to various diseases later in life, such as glucose intolerance and cardiovascular disease.[14] Even though the later generation did not experience famine firsthand, their bodies displayed the effects of malnutrition.

If we can pass on health and emotional benefits and detriments, how could your belief or unbelief impact your children and your children's children from generation to generation?

Luke 11:9–13 says:

"Ask, and it will be given to you; seek, and you will find; knock, and it will be opened to you. For everyone who asks receives, and the one who seeks finds, and to the one who knocks it will be opened. What father among you, if his son asks for a fish, will instead of a fish give him a serpent; or if he asks for an egg, will give him a scorpion? If you then, who are evil, know how to give good gifts to your children, how much more will the heavenly Father give the Holy Spirit to those who ask him!"

When you operate in faith, you leave your children a legacy of success. Even though you may come from nothing, faith can make you something. Let it begin with you.

I have a lot of successful friends. Some grew up with a silver spoon in their mouth, while others came from humble beginnings. But all of them, without exception, give glory to God for their faith and what it has allowed them to do. "God is no respecter of persons" (Acts 10:34 KJV). He sees us all as precious. He sees you for all that you were made to do, for all eternity. If the situation you were born into wasn't all it could have been, you can begin a new generation that chooses to follow Jesus and sows blessings for the generations to come. You can begin a cycle of blessing rather than dysfunction.

Parents who have loved and trained their children well will see their adult children thrive and walk with Christ, as God promises in Proverbs 22:6: "Train up a child in the way he should go; even when he is old he will not depart from it." And Proverbs 23:24–25 says, "The father of the righteous will greatly rejoice; he who fathers a wise son will be glad in him.

Let your father and mother be glad." Children who are loved and valued will honor their parents and pass on their heritage to their own children and grandchildren.

Weapons of War

What are the weapons God has given us to fight off the enemy, to fight off fear, and to turn from sin?

First John 4:4 says, "Greater is He who is in you than he who is in the world" (NASB). Second Corinthians 10:4 says, "The weapons of our warfare are not carnal, but mighty through God to the pulling down of strong holds" (KJV). And Ephesians 6:11 tells us, "Put on the whole armour of God, that ye may be able to stand against the wiles of the devil" (KJV). God tells us to prepare for spiritual warfare. He also tells us what we need to apply the spiritual principles revealed in the Bible.

According to Ephesians 6:10–18, we must:

- Identify the enemy
- Strengthen ourselves in the Lord
- Cover ourselves with the armor of God

God wants to walk with you, lead you, and protect you in everything you do. You are strong in the Lord, so put on the whole armor of God, and pray always. As believers, we have nothing to fear.

It's important to understand what the whole armor of God is and how to use the weapons of war He has given you to live in victory. Prayer is the power that completes the armor and makes it effective against the enemy of our soul.

Seven Pieces of Armor: Seven Weapons of War

Preparing for spiritual warfare requires us to the apply the spiritual principles God tells us about in Ephesians. The armor of God, applied and used properly, provides full protection and enables us to hold our ground against the enemy until we can claim the victory. Two of these weapons—prayer and the sword of the Spirit—are to be used offensively against the enemy. The other weapons listed are to protect us.

Here are the seven pieces of armor described in Ephesians 6:

- The girdle of truth. A battle gear girdle goes around your wait and hips. It protects the region where you generate life. Get the Word deep down inside you and let it hold you up and protect you and speak life over you.
- The breastplate of righteousness. The breastplate covers vital organs, including the heart. The breastplate of righteousness fortifies you and protects your heart against the attacks of the enemy.
- The shoes of peace. They allow you to stand firmly in any situation. You must be grounded on a solid foundation of the gospel of love and peace to attain serenity.

- The shield of faith. With this shield you will be able to quench all the fiery darts of the wicked one. When you are shielded in prayer and in right relationship with God, the schemes of the enemy can't touch you. He can't succeed in revoking God's covenant with you.
- The helmet of salvation. It covers your head, your mind, and your thoughts.
- The sword of the Spirit, which is the Word of God. The Bible is intended to be used as an offensive weapon against the enemy. God's Word protects us against the enemy affecting our mind, heart, walk, actions, nature, character, and life. We are unmovable, unshakable. And because of the truth within, we are able to stand against the enemy.
- Prayer. We are to pray with diligence, perseverance, and supplication, and for those who cannot. Prayer is a sweet perfume that God relishes. It's based on a sacred relationship that thwarts all plots, schemes, and deceptions of the enemy. It allows forgiveness, and it engenders love.

Declare Victory

Now that you see how faith works and what you must do to set your mind and heart to pursue faith, I want to share with you how to declare victory and live every day in faith with the almighty God who created you.

God wants to
walk with you,
lead you,
and protect you
in everything
you do.

Isaiah 54:2–3 says, "'Enlarge the place of your tent, and let the curtains of your habitations be stretched out; do not hold back; lengthen your cords and strengthen your stakes. For you will spread abroad to the right and to the left, and your offspring will possess the nations and will people the desolate cities.'"

Merely trust the Lord and fully apply God's divine law. When you have developed God-like faith, you will be able to affirm the presence and power of God until the very substance of His Spirit in you shows itself.

Proverbs 23:7 says that as we think in our hearts, so we become. Luke 6:45 says that what we speak comes from the heart. The way we think controls what we say and what we become.

If you understand that your words have power, you can bring forth the calling God has placed on your life. You can accomplish all that God has for you to do without fear, anxiety, or dread. God says, "Fear not, for I am with you" (Isaiah 41:10 NKJV). Put that deep in your heart and be assured that things will work out for your good!

In Mark 11:22–24, Jesus said, "'Have faith in God. Truly, I say to you, whoever says to this mountain, "Be taken up and thrown into the sea," and does not doubt in his heart, but believes that what he says will come to pass, it will be done for him. Therefore I tell you, whatever you ask in prayer, believe that you have received it, and it will be yours.'"

Second Thessalonians 1:11 says, "To this end we always pray … that our God may make you worthy of his calling and may fulfill every resolve for good and every work of faith by his power."

When my sister-in-law Victoria and her husband, Joel, needed to expand our church, they went looking for a new location. But the properties they tried to buy kept being snatched up by other bidders. In the natural, they were anxious to close on the properties. But instead of asking, "Why me, God?" Joel and Victoria kept believing that God had something better. They prayed and continued to step out in faith.

Eventually they got an opportunity to purchase a property in Houston that was more than they had expected. Right up to the finish, it was touch and go. But because of their faith and relationship with God, they knew the outcome would be just what they needed. We now have an amazing location in the center of Houston, where hundreds of thousands of people have come to worship and give their lives to Christ.

It could have gone differently if they had started doubting that God wanted them to have a magnificent facility. If they had simply accepted that where we were at that time was all that God had for us, God would not have been able to bring about all that he had in store. Joel and Victoria's faith allowed them to be in full communion with God's will and anointing. The authority of God came through and manifested a bountiful harvest that is still blessing people today.

Second Peter 1:2–4 states, "Grace and peace be multiplied to you in the knowledge of God and of Jesus our Lord. His divine power has granted to us all things that pertain to life and godliness, through the knowledge of him who called us to his own glory and excellence, by which he has granted to us his precious and very great promises, so that through them you may become partakers of the divine nature, having escaped from the corruption that is in the world."

What an exhilarating and freeing state of mind that would be, to fully capture the essence of God's divine relationship with us. To know that every day we can wake up assured that success lies ahead of us because we are His children, because we have a divine nature restored to us for eternity by Jesus' resurrection.

Only through prayer and daily devotion to God's Word can we fully live according to His authority and reap his blessings. All power and might is given to us!

I am often comforted by Isaiah 54:17, which says, "No weapon that is fashioned against you shall succeed, and you shall refute every tongue that rises against you in judgment. This is the heritage of the servants of the LORD and their vindication is from me, declares the LORD." That means the enemy will not prevail against us, and that we can win.

Isaiah 55:11 says, "So shall my word be that goes out from my mouth; it shall not return to me empty, but it shall accomplish that which I purpose, and shall succeed in the thing for which I sent it." We can be assured that what we speak with intent and faith will accomplish its purpose and succeed.

Twenty-One Faith-Filled Affirmations

Here is a twenty-one-day exercise to reinforce your faith. The following passages teach that God has given us a mighty sword that cuts both ways. Our words can be used to deflect the enemy, to provide blessings to ourselves and others, and to bring God's plans for us to successful completion. Through practice and affirmation of faith, we can overcome fear.

Meditate on one of these passages today, thinking about what God is saying to you. The next day, do the same with another passage, and so on for the next twenty-one days until you have worked through all the passages. Also, make the affirmation that follows each scripture your own.

After twenty-one days of devotion and deep reflection, you will feel renewed. God will cause you to see His glory. Your thinking will change, and you will be able to step out in faith to claim your rightful authority in Jesus Christ.

"Blessed is the man [whose] … delight is in the law of the LORD, and in His law he meditates day and night. He shall be like a tree planted by the rivers of water that brings forth its fruit in its season, whose leaf also shall not wither; and whatever he does shall prosper." (Psalm 1:1–3 NKJV)

Affirmation: God, let me walk according to your word so I can bring forth your blessings.

"The LORD has said to Me, 'You are My Son, today I have begotten You. Ask of Me, and I will give You the nations for Your inheritance, and the ends of the earth for Your possession.'" (Psalm 2:7–8 NKJV)

Affirmation: Lord, let me ask you as a child who seeks his parent, knowing you will answer me with your power and authority.

"You, O LORD, are a shield for me, my glory, and the One who lifts up my head. I cried to the LORD with my voice, and He heard me from His holy hill. ... I lay down and slept; I awoke, for the LORD sustained me. I will not be afraid of ten thousands of people who have set themselves against me all around. Arise, O LORD! Save me, O my God!" (Psalm 3:3–7 NKJV)

Affirmation: Lord, I will not be afraid because in you I find strength that sustains me.

"But know that the LORD has set apart for Himself him who is godly; the LORD will hear when I call to Him. ... Put your trust in the LORD. ... I will both lie down in peace, and sleep; for You alone, O LORD, make me dwell in safety." (Psalm 4:3, 5, 8 NKJV)

Affirmation: God, you have set me apart. You hear me and make me feel safe so that I sleep peacefully and rest.

"Let all those rejoice who put their trust in You; let them ever shout for joy, because You defend them; let those also who love Your name be joyful in You. For You, O LORD, will bless the righteous; with favor You will surround him as with a shield." (Psalm 5:11–12 NKJV)

Affirmation: Lord, let your joy dwell in me and the favor of Christ surround me like a shield.

"The LORD has heard the voice of my weeping. The LORD has heard my supplication, the LORD receives my prayer." (Psalm 6:8–9 NASB)

Affirmation: Thank you, Lord, for your mercy. You hear me and comfort me.

"O LORD my God, in you do I take refuge; save me from all my pursuers and deliver me." (Psalm 7:1)

Affirmation: Lord God, I trust you will deliver me from fear, doubt, anxiety, and anything that would persecute me.

"What is man that you are mindful of him, and the son of man that you care for him? Yet you have made him a little lower than the heavenly beings and crowned him with glory and honor. You have given him dominion over the works of your hands; you have put all things under his feet, all sheep and oxen, and also the beasts of the field, the birds of the heavens, and the fish of the sea, whatever passes along the paths of the seas." (Psalm 8:4–8)

Affirmation: Thank you, Lord Jesus, that you created me and that you care enough about me to save me.

With you I have eternal life, power, and authority to overcome all obstacles.

"The LORD is a stronghold … in times of trouble. And those who know your name put their trust in you, for you, O LORD, have not forsaken those who seek you." (Psalm 9:9–10)

Affirmation: You are my strong tower; to you I run and put my faith in your promises knowing that you will help me through all my trials.

"O LORD, you hear the desire of the afflicted; you will strengthen their heart; you will incline your ear." (Psalm 10:17)

Affirmation: O Lord, you are so good to me. You hear me when I am in pain and you answer me with your strength.

"The LORD is righteous; he loves righteous deeds; the upright shall behold his face." (Psalm 11:7)

Affirmation: Lord, I will do as you ask because your judgment is higher than mine, your ways are better than my ways, and in you is all righteousness.

"The words of the LORD are pure words, like silver refined in a furnace on the ground, purified seven times." (Psalm 12:6)

Affirmation: How sweet are your words, Lord. Let me hear you tell me what is right and just and pure.

"I have trusted in your steadfast love; my heart shall rejoice in your salvation. I will sing to the LORD, because he has dealt bountifully with me." (Psalm 13:5–6)

Affirmation: Thank you, Lord, for your unbounded love for me. I rejoice in you always.

"The LORD looks down from heaven on the children of man, to see if there are any who understand, who seek after God." (Psalm 14:2).

Affirmation: I seek you, Lord, because no one else could know me as you do, or understand my heart and deal with me in mercy.

"O LORD, who shall sojourn in your tent? Who shall dwell on your holy hill? He who walks blamelessly and does what is right and speaks truth in his heart." (Psalm 15:1–2)

Affirmation: I want to know you, Lord. I want to live in fellowship with you. Search me, God, and find me worthy of a relationship built on mutual trust.

"The LORD is my chosen portion and my cup; you hold my lot. The lines have fallen for me in pleasant places; indeed, I have a beautiful inheritance. I bless the LORD who gives me counsel; in the night also my heart instructs me. I have set the LORD always before me; because he is at my right hand, I shall not be shaken. Therefore my heart is glad, and my whole being rejoices; my flesh also dwells secure. For you will not abandon my soul to Sheol, or let your holy one see corruption. You make known to me the path of life; in your presence there is fullness of joy; at your right hand are pleasures forevermore." (Psalm 16:5–11)

Affirmation: Almighty God, my praise and glory are yours because my heart is filled with you. You guide me to succeed, you strengthen me, and you fill me with joy.

"You have tried my heart, you have visited me by night, you have tested me, and you will find nothing; I have purposed that my mouth will not transgress." (Psalm 17:3)

Affirmation: As you raise me up, Lord God, search my heart and see that my spirit is filled with you.

"I love you, O LORD, my strength. The LORD is my rock and my fortress and my deliverer, my God, my rock, in whom I take refuge, my shield, and the horn of my salvation, my stronghold. I call upon the LORD, who is worthy to be praised, and I am saved from my enemies." (Psalm 18:1–3)

Affirmation: I love you, Lord. You are my bedrock, my refuge, and my salvation. I have no fear. Your power fills me completely.

"The law of the LORD is perfect, reviving the soul; the testimony of the LORD is sure, making wise the simple; the precepts of the LORD are right, rejoicing the heart; the commandment of the LORD is pure, enlightening the eyes; the fear of the LORD is clean, enduring forever; the rules of the LORD are true, and righteous altogether. More to be desired are they than gold, even much fine gold; sweeter also than honey and drippings of the honeycomb. Moreover, by them is your servant warned. … Let the words of my mouth and the meditation of my heart be acceptable in your sight, O LORD, my rock and my redeemer." (Psalm 19:7–11, 14)

Affirmation: I pray for your wisdom, Lord. Give me discernment and show me how to make good choices. Your words are a sweet delight in my ears and in front of my eyes. Let my words and deeds be blessed in your sight.

"May the LORD answer you in the day of trouble! May the name of the God of Jacob protect you! May he send you help from the sanctuary and give you support from Zion! May he remember all your offerings and regard with favor your burnt sacrifices! … May he grant you your heart's desire and fulfill all your plans! May we shout for joy over your salvation, and in the name of our God set up our banners! May the LORD fulfill all your petitions!" (Psalm 20:1–5)

Affirmation: Grant me the desires of my heart, Lord, that they may fulfill your plans and that you would bless me to be a blessing to others.

"O LORD, in your strength the king rejoices, and in your salvation how greatly he exults! You have given him his heart's desire and have not withheld the request of his lips. For you meet him with rich blessings; you set a crown of fine gold upon his head. He asked life of you; you gave it to him, length of days forever and ever. His glory is great through your salvation; splendor and majesty you bestow on him. For you make him most blessed forever; you make him glad with the joy of your presence. For the king trusts in the LORD, and through the steadfast love of the Most High he shall not be moved." (Psalm 21:1–7)

Affirmation: I pray that my life will be an example of faith, hope, and love; a sweet fragrance to you, my God and Savior; a long life crowned with blessings and glory and love and protection.

12

FAITH IS TRUSTING IN GOD

---○---

"I know the plans I have for you," declares the LORD,
"plans to prosper you and not to harm you,
plans to give you hope and a future."

JEREMIAH 29:11 NIV

Trust is a very personal and intimate thing. When you trust someone, you choose to believe that this person will not do you any harm. You feel safe enough to be vulnerable with him or her, physically and emotionally. There are probably only one or two people you trust completely with every aspect of your heart and life.

You can put all your trust in God even more than your closest friend or family member. He knows you completely, inside and out. He is not willing to walk away from you. He sealed the deal forever when Jesus died on the cross and was resurrected.

God is eager to meet with you and reveal Himself to you. All He asks is that you come to Him just as you are and let Him dwell within you.

God Is Faithful Too

Faith is not a one-way street. God's covenant with us requires Him to be faithful to us as well. First Corinthians 1:9 tells us, "God is faithful, through whom you were called into fellowship with His Son, Jesus Christ our Lord" (NASB). Second Thessalonians 3:3–4 says, "The Lord is faithful. He will establish you and guard you against the evil one. And we have confidence in the Lord."

God's Word is true, and He lives in His Word. He won't violate His covenant with us. He can't. A covenant is a sacred agreement between you and God. It sets specific conditions, and He promises to bless you when you obey those conditions.

Adam sinned and violated the first covenant God made with mankind. But then Jesus came and established a new and everlasting covenant that assures you and me that we have all that God has promised.

How can we develop a faith that conquers fear? Romans 10:17 says, "Faith comes by hearing, and hearing by the Word of God" (NKJV). By carefully studying the Bible, we develop a strong faith. God wants us to know Him and completely rely on his direction in our lives. Through hearing, reading, and meditating on Scripture, we will build a strong, confident faith.

Spending time in prayer and quiet worship develops a relationship with God that will see us through even the darkest times. God will help you leave fear-based thinking behind. He has promised to give each of us a new heart and fresh desires. In Ezekiel 36:26, He says, " 'I will give you a new heart and put a new spirit within you; I will take the heart of stone out of your flesh and give you a heart of flesh' " (NKJV). He wants to give you a heart made in His image, filled with His love and power.

First Peter 3:12 promises, "The eyes of the LORD are on the righteous, and his ears are open to their prayers." James 5:16 says, "The effective, fervent prayer of a righteous man avails much" (NKJV). If you pray powerful, dedicated, fervent, passionate, continuous, persistent prayers, you will see results, just like David did.

Like us, David experienced times of fear. Psalm 56:3 says, "Whenever I am afraid, I will trust in you" (NKJV). Psalm 119 is filled with verses that tell us how David sought after God's Word: "I seek you with all my heart" (v. 10 NIV), "I meditate on your precepts" (v. 15 NIV), and "I have hidden your word in my heart" (v. 11 NIV).

Psalm 91 promises:

Whoever dwells in the shelter of the Most High will rest in the shadow of the Almighty. I will say of the LORD, "He is my refuge and my fortress, my God, in whom I trust." ... He will cover you with his feathers, and under his wings you will find refuge; his faithfulness will be your shield and rampart. You will not fear the terror of night, nor the arrow that flies by day, nor the pestilence that stalks in the darkness, nor the plague that destroys at midday. A thousand may fall at your side, ten thousand at your right hand, but it will not come near you. ... For he will command his angels concerning you to guard you in all your ways. ... "Because he loves me," says the Lord, "I will rescue him; I will protect him, for he acknowledges my name. He will call on me, and I will answer him; I will be with him in trouble, I will deliver him and honor him." (vv. 1–2, 4–7, 11, 14–15, NIV)

According to BibleGateway.com, there are almost 5,500 promises God has made to us to give us a future and a hope.[15] Here are a few things that God promises to us in Scripture. These are things you can pray for and claim victory over with authority and faith:

- Forgiveness
- Money/finances
- Supply
- Healing
- Wisdom/guidance
- Children and family
- Marriage

- Peace
- Overcoming temptation
- Protection
- Fear
- Resurrection
- Eternal life
- End of suffering

You can count on God to keep all His promises. You have a covenant with Him, and even if you break it, He will always come back to you to reestablish a relationship that is holy and filled with His love for you. In Psalm 89:34, He says, "No, I will not break my covenant; I will not take back a single word I said" (NLT).

Second Corinthians 1:20 tells us that God is ready to grant us what we seek: "For all the promises of God in Him are Yes, and in Him Amen, to the glory of God through us" (NKJV).

Now that you have knowledge, trust, and the means to attain all that you desire, how can you achieve your vision?

Write the Plan

Habakkuk 2:2–4 says, "The LORD answered me, 'Write the vision; make it plain on tablets, so he may run who reads it. For still the vision awaits its appointed time; it hastens to the end—it will not lie. If it seems slow, wait for it; it will surely come; it will not delay.'"

Why write down your hopes and wishes? Because that exercise will enable you examine them and set priorities for how you want to accomplish your plan. Let's say you want to take a trip to Europe, and you also want to landscape the backyard. You can only do one of those things at a time. Which will you choose to do first?

List all the steps required to accomplish each one. Start with a budget and a timeline. Consider what you will need to set each plan in motion. Then you can make a decision about which one is the higher priority and whether you have the funds to undertake that task.

Setting out a plan to accomplish your hopes and desires requires a similar process. Write down all the things that make you fearful. Then write down the Scriptures that allow you to overcome those fears. And what you will do to set fear aside. Start speaking prayers and Scripture, affirming what you want from God to help you overcome your fears. See that blessing in your mind's eye, chasing you and overtaking you.

Deuteronomy 28:2 says, "All these blessings shall come upon you and overtake you, if you obey the voice of the LORD your God." If you do this at the beginning of every year, you will accomplish much more than you ever thought you would.

I have had a habit of writing down my goals for the year, doing this since I was in high school. It's a short list of things that are on my heart to do. Some are bucket-list items, while others are just goals that I want to accomplish that year. Sometimes, I write out the list in my iPhone notes, other times on a piece of paper. Sometimes I forget about it for months. But at the end of the year, I look back on the list, and sure enough,

I have accomplished almost all of the big items. It makes me smile and gives me a sense of accomplishment to see what God has done in my life.

He has given me the desires of my heart, sometimes with a few well-earned lessons along the way. What I have learned from writing down my goals is that when we truly walk in faith with Him, He manifests his faithfulness to us.

Once I turn my, "How am I going to get anything done, Lord?" into, "Will you help me get this done, Lord?" the doors open. Taking a step out in faith keeps the stumbling block of fear from freezing me in place and allows me to put my faith into action.

TRUST: Another Word for Faith

Proverbs 3:5 calls on us to "trust in the LORD with all your heart, and do not lean on your own understanding." How do you start believing that what God has for you is success and everlasting life? How can you unlock the power of your faith to receive what God has given you?

The most important thing you can do is trust Him. You may believe that Jesus Christ is your Savior and that God is almighty. But if you don't trust Him with your life, your faith has no power.

Children naturally rely on their parents, and through parents' teaching, children learn how to succeed. Somewhere along the way, children realize that they have to become self-sufficient. Hopefully, based on what they learned growing up, they will make good decisions as adults. Though they may call on their parents or other mentors for advice from time to time, they learn how to do things for themselves.

In the beginning, Adam and Eve had a personal relationship with God, and trusting Him was second nature to them. But when they listened to the enemy's voice, they thought they could make decisions without their Creator. That took them out of their natural relationship with God. They got thrown out of the house too soon, before they had a chance to learn all that God wanted them to learn.

As a result, our decision making is not always in line with our Creator, and so we do not operate in the full power of faith that God has for us. Because we tend to rely on ourselves instead of our faith, we don't know how to fully manifest our faith, power, and love.

Only when we seek God, come under His authority, and learn the lessons of faithfulness, relationship, love, and power can we come into perfect relationship with our Creator. As citizens of His kingdom, we then have the authority to call good things into our lives.

Proverbs 2:1–7 says, "If you receive my words and treasure up my commandments with you, making your ear attentive to wisdom and inclining your heart to understanding; yes, if you call out for insight and raise your voice for understanding, if you seek it like silver and search for it as for hidden treasures, then you will understand the fear of the LORD and find the knowledge of God. For the LORD gives wisdom; from his mouth come knowledge and understanding."

The most
important thing
you can do
is trust Him!

With Your Whole Heart

In Psalm 119, David proclaims to God, "With my whole heart I seek you; let me not wander from your commandments! I have stored up your word in my heart" (vv. 10–11). Near the end of the psalm, he says, "My tongue will sing of your word, for all your commandments are right" (v. 172). The word *heart* is mentioned thirteen times in a positive way in this psalm, emphasizing that David has completely and wholeheartedly given himself to God.

David was chosen by God, and through his experiences he learned to rely on God's Word. Having faith in their relationship allowed him to succeed; without God, he was bound to stumble and flounder.

We often think of David's story the way it was told to us in Sunday school or storybooks. David was a shepherd boy, he threw a rock and killed the Philistine giant, and then he became king of Jerusalem. Instead of settling for the cleaned up children's version, take some time to read the whole story of David in the books of 1 and 2 Samuel and Psalms.

David wasn't just a nice young boy who spent his days tending sheep in the fields. He was a fierce guardian of his flock. He fought off wild animals with his bare hands. His older brothers were soldiers in the king's army who knew how to fight and kill, and David was expected to do the same when the time came. As an adult, David was a rugged, good-looking guy who loved women, and they loved him back. He had several wives and numerous children.

Because David was a fearless warrior, David's father-in-law, the king, was jealous of him—Saul even tried to have him killed on several occasions. (And you thought you had in-law problems!)

David became a seasoned and stalwart fighter for his people, but he knew the Lord, and he never went counter to God's laws. He was loyal, merciful, and fearless throughout this life. What made him successful was the knowledge he had of God and the assurance that he walked in God's anointing and authority. That is what distinguished him from others.

When we read 1 and 2 Samuel and Psalms, we see that David faced many obstacles during his life. He also faced many fears. But he refused to let those fears defeat him. He fought off bears and lions to protect his flock. He slayed a giant armed with nothing but his slingshot. He went to war with the enemies of Israel. Through sickness and disease, through the loss of his best friend Jonathan, and even through the death of his firstborn child, David always turned to God, knowing that his faith and his persistent prayers would be all he needed to see things through.

God will give you the power to do whatever He asks of you. His plans are good, and His promises are always fulfilled in you when you believe. Faith is the key to opening the windows of heaven. We all face moments of fear. But if we get out of the boat and keep our eyes on Him and not on our own strengths, we will pass the test.

Second Corinthians 13:5 says, "Examine yourselves, to see whether you are in the faith. Test yourselves. Or do you

not realize this about yourselves, that Jesus Christ is in you?"
In Ephesians 4:17–24, we are told:

> You must no longer walk as the Gentiles do, in the
> futility of their minds. They are darkened in their
> understanding, alienated from the life of God because
> of the ignorance that is in them, due to their hardness
> of heart. They have become callous and have given
> themselves up to sensuality, greedy to practice every
> kind of impurity. But that is not the way you learned
> Christ!—assuming that you have heard about him
> and were taught in him, as the truth is in Jesus, to put
> off your old self, which belongs to your former man-
> ner of life and is corrupt through deceitful desires,
> and to be renewed in the spirit of your minds, and to
> put on the new self, created after the likeness of God
> in true righteousness and holiness.

We must renew our relationship with God, seek His
anointing, and operate from an open and loving spirit.

I know I keep talking about faith, power, hope, and love,
but it's only because I want you to look at these concepts in
a new way. We have all heard and read these words over and
over again, but often without really understanding what God
wanted us to learn.

He is giving you the keys to operate in power. You can
use these keys to open the windows of heaven. Then, through
faith, you will be able to access all of His promises and

authority. You will be able to cast out fear and darkness, and you will walk in light, power, and love.

Reset Your Inner Voice

You have to calm the inner dialogue and sit in quiet contemplation, seeking to know what God has for you. Romans 12:2 says, "Do not conform to the pattern of this world, but be transformed by the renewing of your mind. Then you will be able to test and approve what God's will is—his good, pleasing, and perfect will" (NIV). This calls for us to renew our minds according to God's will.

First John 5:14–15 says, "This is the confidence that we have toward him, that if we ask anything according to his will he hears us. And if we know that he hears us in whatever we ask, we know that we have the requests that we have asked of him."

Can You Imagine?

Everything we can imagine can become reality. Space exploration, gourmet meals, a medical breakthrough, a beautifully decorated home, self-driving cars, a lovely painting, a novel, a new technology application—each of these things first had to be an idea. Someone had to think about it, research it, pursue it, gather the tools and supplies needed, then try it out, finding what worked and what didn't, until he or she succeeded in creating what was first imagined.

God's Word is like that. If we meditate and pray on it, and have it constantly before us, when challenges come, instead of freezing from fear or falling back on bad habits or hiding away with the covers over our heads, we can choose to believe that God has an answer for us. The path has been clearly defined, and it's in our best interest to pursue His purpose.

How do we know that? Because Romans 8:28 says, "For those who love God all things work together for good, for those who are called according to his purpose." That's a promise from God that allows us to step out and do what we are called to do.

Believing God for His best has changed my life over and over. I pray that as you study His Word and what it means to have faith, God will give you the courage to do all that you could ask or think according to His riches in glory (Ephesians 3:20–21).

In Mark 11:22, Jesus told his followers, " 'Have faith in God.' " Try Him out. Ask Him in faith and authority to work out something in your life that is beyond a natural solution. God is saying to you, "Test me. Put your faith in me. Show me—through something that is of great value to you, such as your income—that you have faith in me to take care of you."

Malachi 3:10 says, "Bring the full tithe into the storehouse. … And thereby put me to the test, says the LORD of hosts, if I will not open the windows of heaven for you and pour down for you a blessing until there is no more need." He knows how important money is in the world. And He is willing to multiply your blessings if you trust Him. All He asks is for you to give him a portion of what you bring in. Try giving 10 percent of your income and see if He doesn't multiply it back to you. His covenant with you says that He will take care of you and never abandon you.

How, when, and where are you going to trust God? What areas of your life will you turn over to Him? Act on your faith, pray, and truly believe that faith can change everything for you. Walk in faith, and carry out the powerful treasure God has put in you to show you the surpassing power that belongs to you if you connect with Him. Be courageous enough to cast out your fears and walk in love, hope, and faith. Then you can do all that God has called you to do and created you to do.

Here is my prayer for you:

Your best days are in front of you. Your spirit is indomitable. You are a lion of Judah! God is taking care of you in every way. May you have memories to bless you, challenges to strengthen you, and victories to encourage you because you are well able to serve Him and to do all that Christ has called you to do!

Pray, fear not, step out in faith, and walk with Jesus Christ, our Lord and Savior.

You've got this!

30 Days of Faith-Filled Devotional Verses

Here are thirty verses to stand on, pray over, and fill your mind with faith so that fear will have no place in your mind and heart.

1. "Do not fear, for I am with you; do not be dismayed, for I am your God. I will strengthen you and help you; I will uphold you with my righteous right hand." (Isaiah 41:10 NIV)

2. Whenever I am afraid, I will trust in you. (Psalm 56:3 NKJV)

3. Do not be anxious about anything, but in every situation, by prayer and petition, with thanksgiving, present your requests to God. And the peace of God, which transcends all understanding, will guard your hearts and your minds in Christ Jesus. (Philippians 4:6–7 NIV)

4. "Peace is what I leave with you; it is my own peace that I give you. I do not give it as the world does. Do not be worried and upset; do not be afraid." (John 14:27 GNT)

5. God has not given us a spirit of fear, but of power and of love and of a sound mind. (2 Timothy 1:7 NKJV)

6. There is no fear in love. But perfect love drives out fear, because fear has to do with punishment. The one who fears is not made perfect in love.
    (1 John 4:18 NIV)

7. When anxiety was great within me, your consolation brought me joy. (Psalm 94:19 NIV)

8. "This is what the LORD says … 'Do not fear, for I have redeemed you; I have summoned you by name; you are mine.'" (Isaiah 43:1 NIV)

9. Anxiety weighs down the heart, but a kind word cheers it up. (Proverbs 12:25 NIV)

10. Even though I walk through the valley of the shadow of death, I will fear no evil, for you are with me; your rod and your staff, they comfort me. (Psalm 23:4)

11. "Have I not commanded you? Be strong and of good courage: do not be afraid; nor dismayed, for the LORD your God is with you wherever you go." (Joshua 1:9 NKJV)

12. "Therefore do not worry about tomorrow, for tomorrow will worry about itself. Each day has enough trouble of its own." (Matthew 6:34 NIV)

13. Humble yourselves, therefore, under the mighty hand of God so that at the proper time he may exalt you, casting all your anxieties on him, because he cares for you.
    (1 Peter 5:6–7)

14. Tell everyone who is discouraged, "Be strong and don't be afraid! God is coming to your rescue." (Isaiah 35:4 GNT)

15. "Do not worry about your life, what you will eat; or about your body, what you will wear. For life is more than food, and the body more than clothes. Consider the ravens: They do not sow or reap, they have no storeroom or barn; yet God feeds them. And how much more valuable you are than birds! Who of you by worrying can add a single hour to your life? Since you cannot do this very little thing, why do you worry about the rest?" (Luke 12:22–26 NIV)

16. The Lord is my light and my salvation—whom shall I fear? The Lord is the stronghold of my life—of whom shall I be afraid? (Psalm 27:1)

17. Cast your cares on the Lord and he will sustain you; he will never let the righteous be shaken. (Psalm 55:22 NIV)

18. Immediately he spoke to them and said, "Take courage! It is I. Don't be afraid." (Mark 6:50 NIV)

19. "Be strong and courageous. Do not be afraid or terrified because of them, for the Lord your God goes with you; he will never leave you nor forsake you." (Deuteronomy 31:6 NIV)

20. "For I am the Lord your God who takes hold of your right hand and says to you, Do not fear; I will help you. Do not be afraid … for I myself will help you," declares the Lord, your Redeemer, the Holy One of Israel. (Isaiah 41:13–14 NIV)

21. God is our refuge and strength, an ever-present help in trouble. (Psalm 46:1 NIV)

22. The LORD is with me; I will not be afraid. What can mere mortals do to me? The LORD is with me; he is my helper. (Psalm 118:6–7 NIV)

23. Fear of man will prove to be a snare, but whoever trusts in the LORD is kept safe. (Proverbs 29:25 NIV)

24. He got up, rebuked the wind and said to the waves, "Quiet! Be still!" Then the wind died down and it was completely calm. He said to his disciples, "Why are you so afraid? Do you still have no faith?" (Mark 4:39–40 NIV)

25. The angel of the LORD encamps around those who fear him, and he delivers them. (Psalm 34:7 NIV)

26. Even if you suffer for doing what is right, God will reward you for it. So don't worry or be afraid of their threats. (1 Peter 3:14 NLT)

27. I prayed to the LORD, and he answered me. He freed me from all my fears. (Psalm 34:4 NLT)

28. "Do not be afraid of them; the LORD your God himself will fight for you." (Deuteronomy 3:22 NIV)

29. Jesus told him, "Don't be afraid; just believe." (Mark 5:36 NIV)

30. I am convinced that nothing can ever separate us from God's love. Neither death nor life, neither angels nor demons, neither our fears for today nor our worries about tomorrow—not even the powers of hell can separate us from God's love. (Romans 8:38–39 NLT)

Notes

1   Nadia Kounang, "What Is the Science behind Fear?" *CNN,* October 29, 2015, cnn. com/2015/10/29/health/science-of-fear/index.html.

2   Signe Dean, "Here's How Long It Takes to Break a Habit, According to Science," *ScienceAlert,* September 24, 2015, http://www.sciencealert.com/here-s-how-long -it-takes-to-break-a-habit-according-to-science.

3   Timothy A. Pychyl, "How Long Does it Really Take to Break a Habit?" *Hopes&- Fears,* http://www.hopesandfears.com/hopes/now/question/216479 -how-long-does-it-really-take-to-break-a-habit.

4   Elliot Berkman, PhD, "How Long Does It Really Take to Break a Habit?" *Hopes&- Fears,* http://www.hopesandfears.com/hopes/now/question/216479-how-long -does-it-really-take-to-break-a-habit.

5   *Oxford Living Dictionaries,* s.v. "forgive," https://en.oxforddictionaries.com /definition/us/forgive.

6   Deborah Headstrom-Page, *From Telegraph to Light Bulb with Thomas Edison: My American Journey* (Colorado Springs, CO: Multnomah Books, 1999), 22.

7   "Ashton Cofer: A Young Inventor's Plan to Recycle Styrofoam," *TED,* March 27, 2017, https://www.ted.com/talks/ashton_cofer_a_young_inventor_s_plan_to _recycle_styrofoam/transcript#t-2340.

8   Neel Burton, MD, "What Are Basic Emotions?" *Psychology Today,* January 7, 2016, https://www.psychologytoday.com/blog/hide-and-seek/201601/what -are-basic-emotions.

9   *Psychology Solution,* July 3, 2017, http://www.psychology-solution.com/anxiety /worry-anxiety-fear-panic.

10   Ibid.

11   *Strong's Concordance,* s.v. "euphrosuné," *Bible Hub,* http://biblehub.com/greek /2167.htm.

12   *Strong's Concordance,* s.v. "simchah," *Bible Hub,* http://biblehub.com/hebrew /8057.htm.

13   *Encyclopedia Britannica,* s.v. "Melchizedek," https://www.britannica.com/biography /Melchizedek.

14   Christopher Wanjek, "Your Diet Affects Your Grandchildren's DNA, Scientists Say," *LiveScience,* July 27, 2017, https://www.livescience.com /21902-diet-epigenetics-grandchildren.html.

15   https://www.biblegateway.com/resources/dictionary-of-bible-themes/5467 -promises-divine.

About the Author

As Senior Advisor, Jackelyn Viera Iloff maintains relationships between Joel Osteen Ministries/Lakewood Church and the Houston, Texas, community, as well as state and national leaders. She directs and empowers a team that implements marketing and social media strategies, event planning, coordination and logistics, and outreach programs. She serves as a spokesperson for Lakewood Church and Joel Osteen Ministries on community and church-related issues. She is an ordained minister at Lakewood Church, the largest congregation in the United States. In this role, she offers spiritual guidance and inspirational messages and is a spokesperson to the church community.

Jackelyn has served at the highest levels of economic development, community outreach, and international policy coalitions as Media Liaison for the Republican National Committee and served as a Reagan administration appointee under the US Secretary of Transportation, Elizabeth Dole. She was Deputy Director of the Office of Special Projects, and developed economic initiatives and trade missions, and was the liaison to a major theme park development with the Secretary of Commerce and Trade Office for Virginia's Governor George Allen. She went on to serve as the Director of

Coalitions for the Bush/Quayle campaign, and was a mid-Atlantic Public Relations Director for KPMG, one of the world's largest professional services companies specializing in accounting, tax, and consulting services—one of the Big Four auditors. She was also a key liaison to The Accountants Coalition whose efforts successfully enacted landmark tort reform legislation.

Jackelyn serves on The Elizabeth Dole Foundation Faith Council and is Ministry Media Liaison to several entertainment leaders. She served as an Executive Advisor for the 18th annual NFL sanctioned Super Bowl Gospel Celebration. Jackelyn is a representative on the Greater Houston Partnership and Houston Pastor's Council. In the past, she spearheaded the anti-trafficking Hope & Freedom Walkathon, and actively collaborates with national, state, and local leaders to bring greater awareness to local issues.